It's never been easier to practise KS3 SPaG!

Knowing your spelling, punctuation and grammar is super important for Key Stage 3.
Luckily, there's enough practice in CGP's 10-Minute Workouts
to make your Year 7 skills SPaG-tastic!

Every Workout covers a mix of spelling, punctuation and grammar questions to put
you through your paces — with one for each week of the school year, you're all set.

Answers are included at the back, along with a handy score sheet to track
your progress. CGP's Workouts are the perfect tool for SPaG success!

How to Use this Book

- This book contains 36 workouts. We've split them into 3 sections — one for each term — with 12 workouts each. There's roughly one workout for every week of the school year.

- Each workout is out of 12 marks and should take about 10 minutes to complete.

- The workouts start with two short warm-up questions, followed by a mixture of spelling, punctuation and grammar questions.

- They progress in difficulty, so they're perfect for ensuring that pupils are getting to grips with the spelling, punctuation and grammar skills they need for Year 7 English.

- The tick boxes on the contents page can help to keep a record of which workouts have been attempted.

- Answers and a score sheet can be found at the back of the book.

Published by CGP
ISBN: 978 1 83774 055 0

Editors: Aimee Ashurst, Keith Blackhall, Siân Butler, Andy Cashmore, Heather Cowley, Emma Duffee, Catherine Heygate, Kirsty Sweetman

With thanks to Becca Clifford and John Sanders for the proofreading.

With thanks to Jade Sim for the copyright research.

Clipart from Corel®

Printed by Elanders Ltd, Newcastle upon Tyne.
Based on the classic CGP style created by Richard Parsons.

Text, design, layout and original illustrations
© Coordination Group Publications Ltd. (CGP) 2023
All rights reserved.

Photocopying this book is not permitted, even if you have a CLA licence.
Extra copies are available from CGP with next day delivery • 0800 1712 712 • www.cgpbooks.co.uk

Contents

Autumn Term

- [ ] Workout 1 2
- [ ] Workout 2 4
- [ ] Workout 3 6
- [ ] Workout 4 8
- [ ] Workout 5 10
- [ ] Workout 6 12
- [ ] Workout 7 14
- [ ] Workout 8 16
- [ ] Workout 9 18
- [ ] Workout 10 20
- [ ] Workout 11 22
- [ ] Workout 12 24

Spring Term

- [ ] Workout 1 26
- [ ] Workout 2 28
- [ ] Workout 3 30
- [ ] Workout 4 32
- [ ] Workout 5 34
- [ ] Workout 6 36
- [ ] Workout 7 38
- [ ] Workout 8 40
- [ ] Workout 9 42
- [ ] Workout 10 44
- [ ] Workout 11 46
- [ ] Workout 12 48

Summer Term

- [ ] Workout 1 50
- [ ] Workout 2 52
- [ ] Workout 3 54
- [ ] Workout 4 56
- [ ] Workout 5 58
- [ ] Workout 6 60
- [ ] Workout 7 62
- [ ] Workout 8 64
- [ ] Workout 9 66
- [ ] Workout 10 68
- [ ] Workout 11 70
- [ ] Workout 12 72

Answers 74

Score Sheet 86

Autumn Term: Workout 1

Warm up

1. In each pair, circle the word that is spelt correctly.

    a) (illegible)   inlegible   b) inprobable   (improbable)

    c) (irrelevant) ilrelevant   d) (informal)   imformal

    (1 mark)

2. Underline the adjective in each sentence.

    Obi was absolutely <u>ravenous</u>.

    Jackie sprinted after the <u>greedy</u> squirrel.

    (1 mark)

3. Circle the two missing capital letters and add the two missing full stops to the passage below.

    The (z)ookeeper tried to make the snake from (z)ambia feel comfortable. she fed it plenty of delicious food and gave it a cuddly bear.

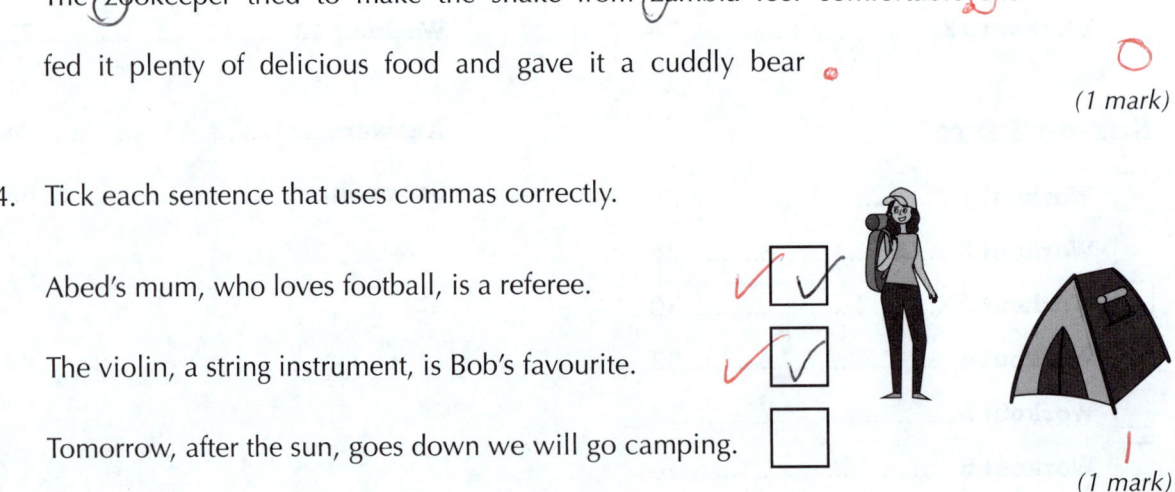

    (1 mark)

4. Tick each sentence that uses commas correctly.

    Abed's mum, who loves football, is a referee. ✓

    The violin, a string instrument, is Bob's favourite. ✓

    Tomorrow, after the sun, goes down we will go camping. ☐

    (1 mark)

5. Write down the subject of each sentence on the lines.

    Rajesh sang the song beautifully.   Rajesh

    Simon was helped by the dentist.   Simon

    (1 mark)

Autumn Term: Workout 1   2   © CGP — not to be photocopied

6. Underline the pronouns in the sentences below.

Debbie wanted to show him some videos, but she accidentally deleted them.

They took the car, parked it at the shop and got me a present.

(2 marks)

7. Rewrite each sentence below, adding a conjunction in the correct place.

Ron wants to ride his bike it's raining.

Ron wants to ride his bike but it's raining.

Paula has eaten a pizza she plans to eat another.

Paula has eaten a pizza and she plans to eat another

(2 marks)

8. Six words with suffixes in this passage are spelt incorrectly.
Rewrite the passage, correcting the mistakes.

> Mizuki was gratefull that her father had agreed to go skydiving. While Mizuki was fearles and loved scary activeties, her father got little enjoiment from them. As the day approached, he looked glumer and more nerveous.

greatfeel✗ (grateful), fearless, enjeryment, approached✗, glummer

activities   nervous

(3 marks)

Score: 8/12

Autumn Term: Workout 2

Warm up

1. In each pair, circle the word that is spelt correctly.
   a) primaryly / (primarily) ✓
   b) (admited) / admitted ✗
   c) (controlling) / controling ✓
   d) miserablely / (miserably) ✓

   (1 mark)

2. Circle the collective noun in each sentence.
   We saw a flock of (geese) raid the corner shop. ✗
   Freya's pack of (wolves) often roamed at night. ✗

   (1 mark)

3. Complete each sentence with the plurals of the words in brackets.
   The wily **foxes** (fox) were friends with the **donkeys** (donkey).
   They disliked the two **wolves** (wolf) who ate their **berries** (berry).

   (1 mark)

4. Tick each sentence that has a relative clause.

   You're the artist who refuses to use the colour purple. ☐ ✓
   After the movie, we are going to play football. ☑
   I bought a hamster that has black and white spots. ☐ ✓

   (1 mark)

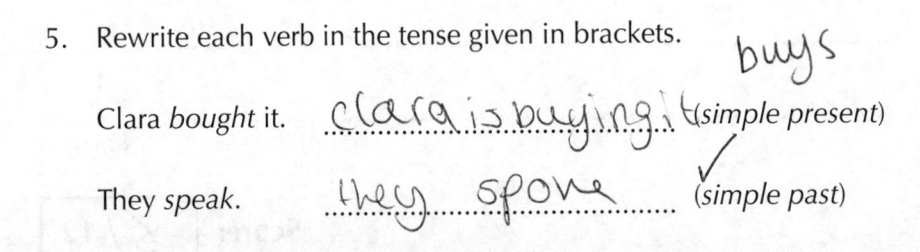

5. Rewrite each verb in the tense given in brackets.

   Clara *bought* it. **Clara is buying it** (simple present) — buys
   They *speak*. **they spoke** (simple past) ✓

   (1 mark)

Autumn Term: Workout 2

6. Underline the correct spelling of the words in bold to complete the sentences.

   The tour guide provided little **assistence** / **assistance**. ✓

   The spider in the bath was an **emergency** / **emergancy**. ✓

   Shanice was a **resident** / **residant** at the lighthouse. ✓

   Louisa was a very **vigilent** / **vigilant** security guard. ✗

   (2 marks)

7. Rewrite the direct speech below so that it is punctuated correctly.

   I enjoyed the sushi said Lucas ✓

   "I enjoyed the sushi," said Lucas.

   The lawyer yelled it's him — the clown is guilty ✓

   The lawyer yelled, "It's him - the clown is guilty!" 2

   (2 marks)

8. Six of the verbs in the passage below are incorrect. Rewrite the passage, correcting the verbs so that they all agree with their subjects.

   > Today we <u>am</u> at the beach — I <u>is</u> having a great time! Jeff made sandwiches, Meera <u>have</u> got a beachball and I <u>has</u> brought towels. It is perfect here — the waves <u>rolls</u> gently and the sun <u>warm</u> us as we <u>sunbathe</u>.

   were ✓   was ✓   had ✓   had ✓   wa~~
   there ✓   warmed ✓   sun bathed ✓

   3

   (3 marks)

   Score: 7 /12

Autumn Term: Workout 3

Warm up

1. Underline the verb in each sentence.

   The expensive planes zoomed over our house.

   Borrow the golden lunchbox next week.

   (1 mark)

2. In each pair, circle the word where the unstressed vowel sound is underlined.

   a) diff<u>e</u>rence   diffe<u>e</u>nce   b) f<u>a</u>ctory   fact<u>o</u>ry

   c) en<u>e</u>mies   <u>e</u>nemies   d) gen<u>e</u>ral   gener<u>a</u>l

   (1 mark)

3. Add 'a', 'an' or 'the' to the sentences below. Use each determiner at least once.

   If you need .... umbrella to avoid .... rain, there are some in the cupboard.

   I wanted to teach her .... lesson about rinsing .... dishes.

   (1 mark)

4. Circle the word that uses an apostrophe incorrectly in each sentence below.

   The girl's thought the children's dolls were creepy.

   Chris's niece liked the dress' colour and pattern.

   Both frogs' tadpoles can be found in the mans' pond.

   (1 mark)

5. Add a prefix to the words in brackets to complete the sentences below.

   Greg .... his broken spatula with a shiny new one. (*placed*)

   Poppy thought golf was fun but Nina .... (*agreed*)

   Grace sped up so she could .... the pedestrians. (*take*)

   Tara wanted to empty the freezer and .... it. (*frost*)

   (2 marks)

6. Underline the preposition in each sentence.

   Ricardo crashed his bike on the way home.

   The grey squirrel leapt over my garden fence.

   Tamsin will be riding Lola's horse until sunset.

   (1 mark)

7. Rewrite the sentences by replacing each underlined phrase with a pronoun.

   <u>Terrance and I</u> chased after <u>those ducks</u>.

   ....

   <u>Rob and Ling</u> built <u>the robot</u> at home.

   ....

   (2 marks)

8. There are six punctuation mistakes in the passage below.
   Rewrite the passage, correcting all of the mistakes.

   > What can you do on a trip to japan. You can eat fresh sashimi (a raw fish dish and take a trip to a Temple in Kyoto. If you enjoy hiking or climbing, there's one place you must go; Mount Fuji All this and much more awaits.

   ....

   ....

   ....

   ....

   ....

   ....

   (3 marks)

   Score: /12

Autumn Term: Workout 4

> **Warm up**
>
> 1. In each pair, circle the word that is spelt correctly.
>
>   a) honest   onest   b) knapkin   napkin
>
>   c) assine   assign   d) descend   desend
>
>   *(1 mark)*
>
> 2. In each pair, underline the sentence that includes an adverb.
>
>   a) Frankie's dress sparkled brightly.   The orange microwave was noisy.
>
>   b) His grey cat is very patient.   Danny will buy the tiny mushroom.
>
>   *(1 mark)*

3. Underline the modal verb in each sentence.

   You must decide which lorry you wish to drive.

   I want to watch a film, but we could go salsa dancing instead.

   (1 mark)

4. Tick each sentence where the subordinate clause is underlined.

   <u>While I go to the gym</u>, Martha will play the piano. ☐

   <u>I didn't enjoy the cheese</u> because it smelt funny. ☐

   Do not open the door <u>until the parrot has been caught</u>. ☐

   (1 mark)

5. Add a prefix to each word so that it has the opposite meaning.

   controlled   ....

   directness   ....

   mature   ....

   (1 mark)

6. Add the six missing commas to the passage below.

   Once the turkey is in the oven we need to boil the carrots the parsnips and the peas. Later on we'll need to roast the potatoes make gravy get the cutlery from the drawer set the table and serve drinks.

   (2 marks)

7. Rewrite the second sentence in each pair by adding a hyphen so that it has the same meaning as the first sentence.

   I need to cover the car again before it snows.
   I need to recover the car before it snows.

   ....

   Watch out for the fish that eats bears.
   Watch out for the bear eating fish.

   ....

   (2 marks)

8. Six verbs in the passage below use tenses incorrectly.
   Rewrite the passage, correcting the verbs so that they use the right tense.

   In my favourite game, you are a robot who is disguising as a human and had to learn about Earth. I buy this game years ago, but I lose my copy. However, I meet the creator yesterday and he gives me a new one!

   ....

   ....

   ....

   ....

   ....

   (3 marks)

   Score: /12

Autumn Term: Workout 5

> **Warm up**
>
> 1. Underline the determiner in each sentence.
>
>   Today, Connor made some cheese.
>
>   We took home four skunks.
>
>   *(1 mark)*
>
> 2. In each pair, underline the sentence that uses contractions correctly.
>
>   a) I willn't go to the circus.   They won't return the carrots.
>
>   b) Guy said he hadn't eaten.   We are'nt allowed to wear tiaras.
>
>   *(1 mark)*

3. Circle the dash that is used incorrectly in each of the sentences below.

   My neighbours — Jen and Marek — like the boats — that sail down the river.

   Millie saw — the clouds — grey and large — were engulfing the sky.

   Gordon — and I made a sandwich — ham and cheese — in the kitchen.

   (1 mark)

4. Add a colon or semicolon in the correct place in each sentence below.

   I'm going to paint a house today Nafula will write a poem about dogs.

   We need a few things a spanner, some nuts and a hammer.

   (1 mark)

5. In each sentence, underline the incorrect homophone.
   Then, write the correct homophone on the line.

   Joanne is off to the market in the mourning.   ....

   Darren isn't aloud to eat peanuts or pineapple.   ....

   I don't know weather to sail home now or later.   ....

   He needs a brake from eating baked beans.   ....

   (2 marks)

6. Draw lines to match each sentence to the correct box.

That film about cowboys was loads of fun!

It was an unsavoury end to the evening.

formal sentence

Ryan may be able to assist you with this.

informal sentence

I was rubbish and blew it for our team.

(1 mark)

7. Rewrite the sentences in the present progressive (continuous) form.

I dive into the custard.

....

We travel to the car wash.

....

(2 marks)

8. There are six spelling mistakes in the passage below.
Rewrite the passage, correcting all of the mistakes.

> A musicion came to our school as a spetial guest. We had a fascinating discusion about her televition appearances. However, I felt frustracian when she signed autographs with just her first inicial and not her whole name.

....

....

....

....

....

(3 marks)

Score: /12

Autumn Term: Workout 6

> **Warm up**
>
> 1. Circle the word that has a hard 'c' in each sentence.
>
>   Naoto carved adorable mice into the celery.
>
>   My chin began to ache after my rugby match.
>
>   *(1 mark)*
>
> 2. In each pair, underline the sentence that includes a possessive pronoun.
>
>   a) We go to Gina's house.   The blue football is hers.
>
>   b) I have two, so use mine.   Vincent wants an apple pie.
>
>   *(1 mark)*

3. Tick each sentence where a clause is underlined.

   On his days off, <u>Riyad gives tours on his fishing boat</u>. ☐

   I always purchase the chilli crisps <u>from the market</u>. ☐

   <u>My cat sleeps</u> for most of the day. ☐

   (1 mark)

4. Choose the correct prefix from the boxes to complete each word.

   | super | inter | photo |

   ....graph   ....market   ....national

   (1 mark)

5. Add three paragraph markers (//) to the passage below.

   It had been a glorious morning when Marcel and Zelda left to go hiking. They had been in high spirits. Three hours later, they were cold, wet and fed up. Marcel's feet ached and his hands were completely numb. "Should we just go home?" he asked. "No, we're nearly at the top of the hill," Zelda said, "so let's keep at it!"

   (1 mark)

6. Add a suffix to each word to turn it into a verb.

   critic .... advert ....

   intense .... glory ....

   (2 marks)

7. Rewrite the list below using bullet points. Use punctuation after each point.

   You will find these things in the attic: a photo album from school, my old Christmas tree, a stamp collection and a vintage television that doesn't work.

   ....

   ....

   ....

   ....

   ....

   (2 marks)

8. There are six places where non-Standard English has been used in the passage below. Rewrite the passage so it only uses Standard English.

   > Last night, me and Jasper watched 'Fairy Hippos 3'. We should of arrived at six, but the bus were late so we had to run quick to get there. We love them films — we been to see every one.

   ....

   ....

   ....

   ....

   ....

   (3 marks)

   Score: ☐ / 12

Autumn Term: Workout 7

Warm up

1. In each pair, circle the word that is spelt correctly.

    a) antike   antique   b) roge   rogue

    c) clog   clogue   d) unique   unike

    (1 mark)

2. Draw lines to match each sentence to the correct box.

    How peculiar that is!

    Stop that albatross at once!   exclamation

    Please watch out for the goat!   command

    What a disgusting pizza it is!

    (1 mark)

3. Use a line (|) to separate the main clause and the subordinate clause in each sentence below.

    Miguel couldn't find his car after he left the theme park.

    Although it is difficult, Parvati enjoys scuba diving.

    We had a picnic before we went to the seaside.

    (1 mark)

4. Add the missing semicolons to the passage below.

    During the day, we'll explore a cave where a troll supposedly lives climb a tower that was built 300 years ago and visit a tavern with a cosy fire.

    (1 mark)

5. Tick each sentence where the preposition refers to place.

    Hattie drives the tractor through the barn. ☐

    Under the mattress, I found hundreds of pounds. ☐

    We couldn't cross the street due to the sheep. ☐

    (1 mark)

Autumn Term: Workout 7   14   © CGP — not to be photocopied

6. Add 'ie' or 'ei' to each of the words below.

   rec……ve   s……ze   bel……ve

   n……ghbour   sh……ld   gr……f

   (2 marks)

7. Rewrite the active sentences below in the passive voice.

   Everyone enjoyed the volleyball match.

   ………………………………………………………………………………………………

   The parrot mocked Helena's singing.

   ………………………………………………………………………………………………

   (2 marks)

8. There are six spelling mistakes in the passage below.
   Rewrite the passage, correcting all of the mistakes.

   > Eric went to see a play about a treazure hunter who goes on an advensure to find a valueable sword. He said the lead actor was barely audable and the story didn't capcher his attention. It sounds like I probably wouldn't enjoy it.

   ………………………………………………………………………………………………

   ………………………………………………………………………………………………

   ………………………………………………………………………………………………

   ………………………………………………………………………………………………

   ………………………………………………………………………………………………

   ………………………………………………………………………………………………

   (3 marks)

   Score: /12

Autumn Term: Workout 8

Warm up

1. Circle the conjunction in each sentence.

   Toby plays the cello while Nayeli sings.

   Wanda took her scooter because the bus was cancelled.

   (1 mark)

2. In each pair, underline the sentence that uses dashes correctly.

   a) I can't see — it's too dark.   My aunt — likes vanilla milkshakes.

   b) Dean is hiding — he's upstairs.   After a workout — she likes potatoes.

   (1 mark)

3. Add the suffix to each word.

   prefer + ing   ....

   refer + ence   ....

   differ + ed   ....

   (1 mark)

4. Underline the correct spelling of the words in bold to complete the sentences.

   Kyle's new house was rather **spaceious / spacious**.

   I had to be **caucious / cautious** when I approached the snake pit.

   Her lovely laughter was **infectious / infecious**.

   Although it was ugly, the doll was **pretious / precious** to him.

   (2 marks)

5. Add a comma to each sentence to change its meaning.

   We had chocolate cheesecake and popcorn for dinner.

   It is time to go downstairs and eat Katy.

   I bought a radish and some glue for my art project.

   (1 mark)

6. Complete each sentence by using the word in brackets to form a comparative or superlative. You will need to add 'more', 'most' or a word ending.

   Gabby has the .... (*modern*) phone out of us all.

   His jumper is .... (*bright*) than mine.

   Betty is the .... (*lazy*) dog I know.

   (1 mark)

7. Rewrite the sentences below, adding an adverbial phrase to each one.

   Zara hit the ball.

   ....

   We watched the ballet dancer.

   ....

   (2 marks)

8. All of the apostrophes are missing from the passage below. Rewrite the passage, adding all the missing apostrophes.

   > Ryu couldnt believe his ticket was gone. So was Edgars. Iriss too. Hed had them safe in his pocket, but now theyd vanished. He tried not to think about his two friends disappointment.

   ....

   ....

   ....

   ....

   ....

   (3 marks)

   Score: /12

Autumn Term: Workout 9

Warm up

1. Underline the relative pronoun in each sentence.

   Kim is a talented chef who cooks the best pies.

   The koala climbs up the tree that the bird is in.

   (1 mark)

2. In each group of words, circle the word that is not part of the same word family as the other words.

   a) playful   plaid   unplayable

   b) grating   gracious   gratitude

   (1 mark)

3. Tick each sentence where the underlined words form an expanded noun phrase.

   There's <u>a monkey with a hat</u> dozing on the roof. ☐

   I saw <u>the impressive runner training</u> on the track. ☐

   <u>My racket with green stripes</u> is my lucky charm. ☐

   (1 mark)

4. Add inverted commas in the correct places to the sentences below.

   The captain said , Head to that island over there .

   Casper refuses to fly to Chile ! complained Jasminda.

   (1 mark)

5. Circle the comma that is used incorrectly in each of the sentences below.

   Although it had snowed, we still had to go to school, the next day.

   Robert is only packing, a jumper, two pairs of trainers and hair gel.

   Inside, the tunnel, a lorry was stuck and the cars couldn't get past it.

   (1 mark)

6. Underline the adverb in each sentence.
   Write whether it is showing time, place or cause on the lines.

   The moles dug underground.   ....

   Today, I danced on the beach.   ....

   I lost it, therefore I can't return it. ....

   (2 marks)

7. Rewrite the sentences below using the present perfect form.

   Sully leapt over the puddle.

   ....

   You chose the purple curtains.

   ....

   (2 marks)

8. There are six spelling mistakes in the passage below.
   Rewrite the passage, correcting the mistakes.

   > It had been a tuff day on the farm. Not only had the pluogh broken, but the oxes had escaped from their encloshure too. Furthermore, the calfs had faught one another all afternoon.

   ....

   ....

   ....

   ....

   ....

   (3 marks)

   Score: /12

Autumn Term: Workout 10

Warm up

1. In each pair, underline the sentence that uses commas correctly.

    a) Maggie, the mechanic, is very kind.   Maggie, the mechanic is very, kind.

    b) My, sweets, that are sour are cheap.   My sweets, that are sour, are cheap.

    (1 mark)

2. In each pair, circle the word with the correct prefix.

    a) antidote   interdote   b) antipilot   autopilot

    c) intersonic   supersonic   c) superact   interact

    (1 mark)

3. Add a colon in the correct place in each sentence below.

    I am feeling really concerned Isaac twisted his ankle playing softball.

    The gym is closing everyone stopped going there because of the bats.

    (1 mark)

4. Tick each sentence which uses the subjunctive form.

    If I were you, I would stay away from the laboratory. ☐

    You must ensure that Valerie hands in her homework. ☐

    It is vital that Hamza feed the budgie properly. ☐

    (1 mark)

5. Make the sentences less certain by adding a different modal verb to each one.

    We .... tour the country in a van.

    They .... yodel as part of Jamal's song.

    (1 mark)

Autumn Term: Workout 10

6. Underline the correct spelling of the words in bold to complete the sentences.

   A very nasty **scent / sent** was coming from the bin.

   Angela **tipically / typically** dances to music in the morning.

   Hank wanted to paint his bedroom walls **beige / baige**.

   We had to keep my little brother **ocuppied / occupied**.

   (2 marks)

7. Rewrite the sentences, replacing the underlined words with synonyms.

   The scary television programme was boring.

   ....

   Her strong kick is incredible.

   ....

   (2 marks)

8. There are six verbs in the passage below that use the passive voice.
   Rewrite the passage so that it uses the active voice.

   > The explorers were chilled by the blizzard and their dogs were deafened by the wind. The path was shrouded in snow; the ground was covered by ice. The compass was analysed by Wendy, but she was distracted by Jed falling over.

   ....

   ....

   ....

   ....

   ....

   (3 marks)

   Score: ☐ /12

Autumn Term: Workout 11

Warm up

1. Draw lines to match each word to the correct box.

   vehicle
   sadness   concrete noun
   mascot
   victory   abstract noun

   (1 mark)

2. In each pair, circle the word that is spelt correctly.

   a) sleepyness   sleepiness   b) adoration   adoreation

   c) amusement   amusment   d) quized   quizzed

   (1 mark)

3. Circle the word that has the wrong prefix in each sentence below.

   Cameron misregarded my advice to take a detour.

   The robber failed to deable the impressive alarm.

   Ofentse misjudged the challenge, but undercame it anyway.

   (1 mark)

4. Tick each sentence where the underlined adverb shows how possible something is.

   My niece's dog has an <u>extremely</u> loud howl. ☐

   It's <u>likely</u> that the tree will fall down in the storm. ☐

   Matteo likes to bake, so he's <u>probably</u> in the kitchen. ☐

   (1 mark)

5. Rewrite this sentence so that it is more formal.

   Thomas will see you at the party tonight, won't he?

   ....

   (1 mark)

6. Underline the mistake in each sentence. Write the correct spellings on the lines.

   I was bewitched by the glamourous city life. ....

   He'll simplefy the dance for beginners. ....

   The lawyer will advize you how to proceed. ....

   (2 marks)

7. Rewrite each pair of sentences as one sentence by adding a suitable conjunction.

   My dog is small. She's stronger than you think.

   ....

   The soup was cold. He put it in the microwave.

   ....

   (2 marks)

8. There are six punctuation marks missing from the passage below. Rewrite the passage, adding the missing punctuation.

   > My friends — Ellie and Jo are models. My tickets to their fashion show didnt arrive, so Jos parents resent them to me. At the show, Ellie and Jo wore many outfits dresses made from emeralds; some dungarees and long ball gowns.

   ....

   ....

   ....

   ....

   ....

   ....

   (3 marks)

   Score: ☐ /12

Autumn Term: Workout 12

Warm up

1. Underline the pronoun in each sentence.

   Melokuhle wanted to show us the music shop.

   Jacob has an extra umbrella, so Moesha will borrow his.

   (1 mark)

2. Draw lines to show whether each conjunction expresses time, place or cause.

   He went home while it was still light.

   The fire engine is delayed because there's traffic.

   Sandy goes on holiday wherever there is a beach.

   No one leaves until we find the parsnips!

   time

   place

   cause

   (1 mark)

3. Write down the adjective in each sentence on the lines.

   Her sapphire paint spilt everywhere. ....

   Italian food is unbelievably delicious. ....

   They sold the abandoned warehouse. ....

   (1 mark)

4. Circle the semicolon which is used incorrectly in each of the sentences below.

   Bella wanted to go; to the desert; Cid insisted on visiting the rainforest.

   The milk; in the fridge was smelly; the beef was still fresh.

   Zuri is weary; Mona is feeling wide awake; after a good night's sleep.

   (1 mark)

5. Add the correct silent letter to complete each word.

   ans......er   crum......   ......night

   bu......cher   ca......ming   bisc......it

   (2 marks)

6. Underline the verb in each sentence which does not agree with its subject.

   They asks for pepperoni, but I want pineapple on my pizza.

   Ralph play snooker on Tuesdays and naps when he returns home.

   We are worried about going on the ride because it go very fast.

   (1 mark)

7. Rewrite the second sentence in each pair, adding a comma so that it has the same meaning as the first sentence.

   Wilson stole three items from the shop.
   Wilson stole silver earrings and rings from the shop.

   ....

   The speaker tells Julia that Jess is going to cook.
   Jess is now going to cook Julia.

   ....

   (2 marks)

8. There are six spelling mistakes in the passage below. Rewrite the passage, correcting the mistakes.

   > The existance of aliens has been widely dissputed. However, there's some expectency that we'll eventualy discover life forms in space. Currantly though, there is no reliable evidance that aliens exist.

   ....

   ....

   ....

   ....

   ....

   (3 marks)

   Score: ☐ / 12

Spring Term: Workout 1

Warm up

1. Circle the word that is spelt incorrectly in each sentence.

   The invention was of little use to the magicion.

   My obsesion with the new version of the game worried Mike.

   (1 mark)

2. In each pair, underline the sentence that uses brackets correctly.

   a) The jeans (the white ones) are gone.   The baby (escaped) from the cot.

   b) His mum (likes to watch) basketball.   She cooked lunch (for both of them).

   (1 mark)

3. Add a dash to each sentence to separate the main clauses.

   Khalid didn't order the steak he is vegetarian.

   Let's go to watch the roller derby it starts at four.

   Agnes was on the news she saved a swan.

   (1 mark)

4. Add an adverb to each sentence. Use a different adverb in each sentence.

   Jenny .... went to the ice-cream parlour.

   Ivan was .... sad that his package hadn't arrived.

   Olivia is .... waiting for the tiger to wake up.

   (1 mark)

5. Complete each sentence using the present perfect form of the verb in brackets.

   We .... a baby alligator. (*to hold*)

   They .... off the shelf. (*to fall*)

   (1 mark)

6. Rewrite each statement so that it is a question.

   The rugby match is called off.

   ....

   Samir and Ayesha are staying in tonight.

   ....

   (2 marks)

7. Underline the correct spelling of the words in bold to complete the sentences.

   George took some medication to **lessen / lesson** the pain.

   It was **plane / plain** to see that the ship had left without them.

   Alexis took a big **piece / peace** of cake to the table.

   The famous singer was the little girl's **idle / idol**.

   (2 marks)

8. There are six examples of informal language in the passage below. Rewrite the passage, changing the informal words or phrases so that they use formal language.

   > Justin was bang out of order! I am shocked that he hasn't apologised to Kurt for chucking his bag into the river. It was just so uncalled for, right? If I was him, I would get Kurt a prezzie too.

   ....

   ....

   ....

   ....

   (3 marks)

   Score: /12

Spring Term: Workout 2

Warm up

1. In each group of words, circle the word where the 'ough' makes a different sound to the other words.

   a) cough   dough   though

   b) bought   thorough   nought

   (1 mark)

2. Draw lines to match each word to the correct box.

   very | modal verb | rarely

   will | adverb | shall

   (1 mark)

3. Underline the relative clause in each sentence below.

   That is the gentle rhino whose name I have forgotten.

   Julie wants to buy that guitar which is signed by the rock star.

   We found the last chocolate egg Didier had hidden.

   (1 mark)

4. Add the missing comma to each sentence below.

   Before we catch the train we need to buy a ticket.

   While Tonya went to find Bongani I called the lion-tamer.

   Because of the tornado warning it was advised that we all stay at home.

   (1 mark)

5. Tick each sentence that uses the past progressive (continuous) form.

   The doctors were trying to find the lollipops. ☐

   Lara is flying to Barbados with her sisters. ☐

   I heard Bill was swimming with sharks. ☐

   (1 mark)

6. Circle two missing capital letters and add four missing punctuation marks to the text below.

   To decorate my bedroom, I want

   - A large, green beanbag;

     some silver photo frames to hang on the wall

   - a poster of my favourite band

   (2 marks)

7. Expand the noun phrases by adding an adjective and preposition phrase to each one.

   the unusual tree

   ....

   my nephew's garage

   ....

   (2 marks)

8. There are six spelling mistakes in the passage below. Rewrite the passage, correcting all of the mistakes.

   > I thought I was acquireing a relieble table, but I was incorrect. The top was extremely flexable and the legs collapseed constantly. The company are offerring me a refund, but I would have preferred a differrent table.

   ....

   ....

   ....

   ....

   ....

   (3 marks)

   Score: /12

Spring Term: Workout 3

Warm up

1. In each pair, circle the word that is spelt correctly.

    a) plack   plaque   b) moustashe   moustache

    c) chaotic   khaotic   d) critike   critique

    (1 mark)

2. Underline the superlative in each sentence.

    The hot-air balloon ride is the greatest prize in the raffle.

    The tiny mouse was the least intimidating creature Omar had ever seen.

    (1 mark)

3. Choose the correct prefix from the boxes to complete each word.

    | un | | re | | mis |

    ....cede   ....fortune   ....natural

    (1 mark)

4. Tick each sentence that uses pronouns correctly.

    Satoshi and I hurried into the secret base. ☐

    We can't believe them stole the food. ☐

    Rosa and the spy, Clive, met me in a garden. ☐

    (1 mark)

5. Add a pair of dashes in the correct places in the sentences below.

    Klara asked Joy a builder to fix the broken chimney.

    I rolled two and six my favourite numbers on the dice.

    (1 mark)

6. Underline the mistake in each sentence. Write the correct spellings on the lines.

   I got a bruse on my ankle when playing hockey. ....

   She does yoga in her lesure time after work. ....

   We'll perswade them to allow us onto the yacht. ....

   (2 marks)

7. Rewrite the sentences below, adding a preposition phrase to show when the events happen.

   The fireworks were set off.

   ....

   Murni was exhausted.

   ....

   (2 marks)

8. There are six punctuation marks missing from the passage below. Rewrite the passage, adding the missing punctuation.

   "I can honestly say" said Noah, "that this is the hottest Ive ever been."

   Janine replied, "You're being so dramatic, don't you think"

   Can you both stop complaining, snapped Kamil "It's getting on my nerves."

   ....

   ....

   ....

   ....

   ....

   ....

   (3 marks)

   Score: /12

Spring Term: Workout 4

Warm up

1. Underline the object in each sentence.

   The scientists have discovered a new element.

   The sneaky rabbit hides the phone.

   (1 mark)

2. In each pair, circle the word that is spelt correctly.

   a) measure   meazure   b) teacher   teature

   c) frachure   fracture   d) composure composhure

   (1 mark)

3. Tick each sentence that uses a conjunction.

   I spotted a woodpecker sitting on the garden fence. ☐

   Even though Andi was hungry, she shared half of her crisps. ☐

   Jonny hates early starts, yet he got up at 5 am to catch a flight. ☐

   (1 mark)

4. Add a semicolon in the correct place in each of the sentences below.

   Meg will get a taxi home Pedro plans to use an electric scooter.

   The swimming pool was packed the golf course was empty.

   (1 mark)

5. Circle the correct pronoun in bold to complete the sentences.

   Jimmy and Nora went to the cafe so **he / they** could both eat.

   The group was upset that the owner asked **them / we** to leave.

   I took Spot to the park and she chased **I / me** around.

   The woman offered to help me when **she / her** saw I was lost.

   (2 marks)

6. Write the plural of each word below.

woman .... quiz ....

goose .... disco ....

(1 mark)

7. Rewrite the sentences, replacing the underlined words with antonyms.

The <u>delicious</u> pasta was <u>enjoyable</u> to eat.

....

My <u>soft</u> pillow's pattern is very <u>beautiful</u>.

....

(2 marks)

8. The sentences below are in the wrong order.
Split the sentences into three paragraphs so the passage makes sense.

> Rafiq finally arrived in the stadium.
> She always waved to him before kick-off.
> "Go on, Trudy!" yelled Rafiq as the game began.
> He quickly found his seat as the players appeared.
> On the pitch, Trudy, Rafiq's partner, waved.

....

....

....

....

....

....

(3 marks)

Score: /12

Spring Term: Workout 5

Warm up

1. In each pair, circle the word that is spelt correctly.

   a) kords   chords   b) cylinder   sylinder

   c) persent   percent   d) obscure   obskure

   (1 mark)

2. Underline the two verbs in each sentence.

   A full moon occurs when the Earth is between the Sun and the Moon.

   I told you about the wet floor earlier and you still slipped.

   (1 mark)

3. Add either 'tial' or 'cial' to complete the words below.

   poten..........   provin..........

   offi..........   torren..........

   (1 mark)

4. Tick each sentence where the main clause is underlined.

   Avery hid under the covers <u>until the ghost went away</u>. ☐

   While I waited for the bus, <u>I sent Trevor a text</u>. ☐

   <u>Mila brought the raisins</u> that we needed for the cake. ☐

   (1 mark)

5. Rewrite the sentences using direct speech.

   Ching-He asked where the scissors were kept.

   ....

   Anita said she put the biscuits in the tin.

   ....

   (2 marks)

6. Complete the sentences using a conjunction which has a similar meaning to the one in brackets.

   Paige has no more satsumas .... she ate them all. *(for)*

   The book had a sad ending .... we liked it anyway. *(yet)*

   (1 mark)

7. Rewrite the second sentence in each pair, adding one hyphen so that it has the same meaning as the first sentence.

   Is this a party for people who are nearly one hundred?
   Is this a party for ninety eight-year-olds?

   ....

   The day was saved because of a teacher that acted quickly.
   A fast acting teacher saved the day.

   ....

   (2 marks)

8. There are six punctuation marks missing from the passage below. Rewrite the passage, adding the missing punctuation.

   Enoki Cafes menu will warm you up: theres soup served with our bread (it's award-winning!; roast dinners with all the trimmings jacket potatoes with a hot filling of your choice various side dishes and a selection of drinks.

   ....

   ....

   ....

   ....

   ....

   ....

   (3 marks)

   Score: /12

Spring Term: Workout 6

Warm up

1. Tick the sentence that has used a comma correctly.

   After school I am, going to see my grandparents. ☐

   When she is on holiday, Aliyah takes lots of photographs. ☐

   (1 mark)

2. Underline the adverb in each sentence below.

   Felicity often went for a walk in the park.

   Callum felt the yoga class wasn't going well.

   (1 mark)

3. Add 'a', 'an' or 'the' to the sentences below. Use each word once.

   If you're finding it to be .... challenge, ... best person to ask is Arjun. He is .... excellent source of information.

   (1 mark)

4. Circle the correct spelling of the words in bold to complete each sentence below.

   That is some very expensive **jewellery** / **jewllry** .

   I **definately** / **definitely** left the keys on the table.

   Did you chop the **vegtables** / **vegetables** ?

   (1 mark)

5. Rewrite each verb in the tense given in brackets.

   We *ate*. .... (simple present)

   It *breaks*. .... (simple past)

   (1 mark)

6. Add a colon to the correct place in the sentences below.

   Jake had a problem he did not know what he needed to do.

   Aarav was terrified he'd just seen a gigantic spider.

   I have holiday plans I will visit France and Belgium.

   There are two kinds of tree deciduous and coniferous.

   (2 marks)

7. Add a suffix to the words in brackets to complete the sentences below.

   It was very .... of you to drop the plates. *(care)*

   This multi-purpose tool will be very .... *(use)*

   The cat's .... meant she didn't play with toys. *(lazy)*

   I have sent you an .... to my party. *(invite)*

   (2 marks)

8. There are six spelling mistakes in the passage below.
   Rewrite the passage, correcting the mistakes.

   > Gwen is an ambicious writer. She wrote a gloryous story about meeting a ferotious crocodile — it sounded very perilus. I'm suspitious when she says it's entirely fictional as she is always doing outragous things.

   ....

   ....

   ....

   ....

   ....

   (3 marks)

   Score: /12

Spring Term: Workout 7

Warm up

1. Underline the preposition in each sentence.

   a) We sent a postcard from Copenhagen.

   b) There is a family of monsters living under my bed.

   (1 mark)

2. In each pair, circle the word that is spelt correctly.

   a) freit   freight   b) address   adress

   c) crescent   cresent   d) reygn   reign

   (1 mark)

3. Rewrite the sentence below so that it is punctuated correctly.

   leo will make a meal from noodles chicken onion and peppers

   ....

   ....
   (1 mark)

4. Tick each sentence which is written in Standard English.

   It was clear what had happened. ☐

   That's where you've went wrong. ☐

   I done the work you asked me to. ☐

   (1 mark)

5. Rewrite each word on the line with the correct spelling.

   releif   ....

   ceeling   ....

   fearce   ....

   (1 mark)

6. Add commas in the correct places in the sentences below.

The Isle of Man, located in the Irish Sea, is a beautiful place.

The coin, which was later confirmed to be ancient, was found here.

Arthur, my second cousin once removed, turns three today.

Dr Sato, a respected astronomer, announced her new discovery.

(2 marks)

7. Underline the word that is spelt incorrectly in each sentence below. Then, write the correct spelling of the word on the line.

The answer was on the tip of my tung. ....

The bouteek sells lovely clothes. ....

The mosk is near the bakery. ....

The runners were overcome with fatige. ....

(2 marks)

8. There are six phrases in this passage that can be shortened using an apostrophe. Rewrite the passage, replacing these phrases with the shortened forms.

> There is a dance competition that my friend Caitlin and I are planning to enter. She is really good, so I am glad we are performing together. The competition is not until August, so we have got plenty of time to practise.

....

....

....

....

....

(3 marks)

Score: /12

Spring Term: Workout 8

Warm up

1. Circle the word in each pair that uses the 'un-' prefix correctly.

    a) unvalid   unravel   b) unclean   unperfect

    c) unknown   unmobile   d) unmature   unequal

    (1 mark)

2. Underline the adverbial phrase in each sentence.

    The squirrel scampered away very quickly.

    There was water covering the sand as far as the eye could see.

    (1 mark)

3. Use a line (|) to separate the main clause and the subordinate clause in the sentences below.

    Eat your lunch before it gets cold.

    We're going to be late unless we hurry up.

    You can watch the film after you finish your geography homework.

    (1 mark)

4. Tick each sentence that uses commas correctly.

    We bought some brown paper, string, sticky tape, envelopes and a card. ☐

    Rocks shells, stamps, and socks are some of the things Ibrahim collects. ☐

    The nature reserve is home to puffins, barn owls and gannets. ☐

    (1 mark)

5. Complete the table below by correctly adding each suffix to the root words.

Root word	-ed	-ing
knit		
decide		
query		

(2 marks)

Spring Term: Workout 8

6. Add 'who', 'whose' or 'that' to the sentences below. Use each pronoun once.

   There goes the monkey .... stole my bread!

   Denis is the person .... is training to be a plumber.

   He spoke to the man .... car had been stolen.

   (1 mark)

7. Complete the sentences below by writing the correct form of the verb in brackets.

   It was busy when I .... the tickets. (*collect / collects / collected*)

   Ice forms when water .... (*freezes / froze / frozen*)

   We sat and .... about what to do next. (*think / thinks / thought*)

   The cup in the sink has .... (*break / broke / broken*)

   (2 marks)

8. There are six spelling mistakes in the passage below.
   Rewrite the passage, correcting all of the mistakes.

   > The magician brout out a box from behind a curtain and stepped inside with a sense of mystary. After ruffly ten seconds, he was gone! I was intriged since there was no explanasion for this incredible illution.

   ....

   ....

   ....

   ....

   ....

   ....

   (3 marks)

   Score: /12

Spring Term: Workout 9

Warm up

1. In each pair, circle the word that is spelt correctly.

   a) clasify   classify   b) expertise   expertese

   c) intensefy   intensify   d) theorise   theoryse

   (1 mark)

2. In each pair, underline the option that is a phrase.

   a) Eddie's rusty unicycle   Daisy dislikes the smell of bubblegum

   b) there are two wishing wells   the odd lorry with the purple lights

   (1 mark)

3. Tick each sentence where the conjunction shows time.

   I hadn't been to the museum since I was a child. ☐

   Denise practised her oboe before the concert began. ☐

   Gareth was late to the party as he was stuck in traffic. ☐

   (1 mark)

4. Add a determiner to each sentence. Don't use 'a', 'an' or 'the'.

   I am going to see .... hippos at the zoo.

   They searched for .... comic in the living room.

   (1 mark)

5. Cross out a comma in each sentence to change its meaning.
   The sentence should still make sense.

   At the shop, we bought a lemon, jelly and baklava.

   Before painting, Hiromi, Lee and Tori got the brushes out.

   Kabir, an explorer, sprinted after the robber, holding his sack of gems.

   (1 mark)

6. Underline the modal verbs in the sentence below. Then, rewrite the sentence, making it less certain by using different modal verbs.

   I shall bring batteries and Marie will find a screwdriver.

   ....

   ....
   (2 marks)

7. Rewrite the sentences below, adding brackets in the correct places.

   Dustin and Shani a teacher play baseball.

   ....

   The pie was fresh it was made that morning.

   ....
   (2 marks)

8. Six words in the passage below are missing silent letters.
   Rewrite the passage, correcting all of the mistakes.

   > Caleb claimed that he was psycic, but I was doutful. He rinkled his brow and told me a gastly spirit was searching for me. I stopped lisening, but Caleb has a nack for making me worry...

   ....

   ....

   ....

   ....
   (3 marks)

   Score: /12

Spring Term: Workout 10

Warm up

1. Circle the proper nouns in each sentence.

   He is taking Daphne and a troupe of performers to Zimbabwe.

   Warmth finally arrives in Cambridge around May, I have found.

   (1 mark)

2. In each pair, underline the sentence that uses an apostrophe correctly.

   a) Her two kiwi's were crushed.   The men's suits are not stylish.

   b) Otis's surfboard snapped in half.   The boxes's lids had been ripped open.

   (1 mark)

3. Underline the subordinate clause in each sentence.

   As a result of the strike, no helmets will be made in the factory.

   Dani wants to swim to the island even though it is far away.

   Robin will visit the historic site where the famous battle took place.

   (1 mark)

4. Write down the sentence type of each sentence below.

   Drop the gravy granules immediately.   ....

   How fiercely he complained!   ....

   That was such a dreadful roast dinner.   ....

   (1 mark)

5. Circle the dash that needs removing from each sentence.

   The crow was very clever — it distracted the man and — stole his bagel.

   The biscuits — Pippa brought were vile — they tasted incredibly salty.

   My uncle loves visiting — he plays — in the garden with our dog.

   (1 mark)

6. Add either 'ssion', 'sion', 'cian' or 'tion' to complete the words below.

   occa............   politi............   percu............

   fic............   se............   fric............

   (2 marks)

7. Underline the spelling mistakes. Rewrite the sentences with the correct spellings.

   There was a reasonable growth in attendence today.

   ....

   His performance was believeble and confidant.

   ....

   (2 marks)

8. Rewrite the passage below so it is in the simple past tense.

   > Karim goes to the book signing in London and speaks to his fans. He has a great time until one couple asks him for a picture. He gets up to join them, but accidentally spills his coffee all over himself.

   ....

   ....

   ....

   ....

   ....

   (3 marks)

   Score: / 12

Spring Term: Workout 11

Warm up

1. Circle the possessive pronouns and underline the relative pronouns.

   who   theirs   which   ours

   (1 mark)

2. In each pair, circle the word that is spelt correctly.

   a) hidious   hideous   b) furious   furyous

   c) humorous   humourous   d) couragous   courageous

   (1 mark)

3. Underline the correct spelling of the words in bold to complete the sentences.

   She told me her **preference / preferrence** of pie filling.

   Femi was **refering / referring** to the wrong theme park timetable.

   The video **buffered / bufferred** for what seemed like an eternity.

   The **referee / referree** was annoyed at the crowd yelling at her.

   (2 marks)

4. Complete each sentence below by using the word in brackets to form a comparative or superlative. You will need to add 'less', 'least' or change the word in brackets.

   This movie is .... (*interesting*) than the one about cyclones.

   Robyn sat in the .... (*comfortable*) chair in the house.

   Their team did .... (*bad*) on the quiz.

   (1 mark)

5. Add a word to each sentence so that it uses the subjunctive.

   If I .... an engineer, I would create a mechanical dog.

   It is important that he .... the front door shut.

   (1 mark)

Spring Term: Workout 11

6. Underline the longest noun phrase in each sentence below.

My younger brother heard about that girl with the terrific tennis serve.

Some really annoying dogs keep stealing my sausage rolls.

His aunty's massive model train set won praise from fellow enthusiasts.

(1 mark)

7. Rewrite the sentences below, adding a preposition phrase to each one.

The werewolf howled.

....

Joseph climbed the tree.

....

(2 marks)

8. There are six punctuation marks missing from the passage below. Rewrite the passage, adding the missing punctuation.

> What a bizarre day that was On my way to town a car crashed into a pet shop. There were animals everywhere: two dogs, both greyhounds sprinted away; a flock of budgies took flight and a cat sauntered off Do you think they will all be found

....

....

....

....

....

....

(3 marks)

Score: /12

Spring Term: Workout 12

Warm up

1. Circle the comma that needs removing from each sentence.

   My friends, an astronaut and an estate agent, both love, large spaces.

   The two parrots, which have green feathers, and red beaks, are from Africa.

   (1 mark)

2. In each pair, underline the sentence that uses a subordinating conjunction.

   a) I'll buy a pony and he can ride it.   While it's raining, let's make pancakes.

   b) Fay will sleep if we sing softly.   Lev didn't swim nor did he like cycling.

   (1 mark)

3. Add the suffix to each root word and write the new word on the line.

   realise + ation   ....

   timely + ness   ....

   home + less   ....

   (1 mark)

4. Tick each sentence where the adverb shows when things happen.

   The train is due to arrive late.   ☐

   Felix can hear the zombies moving nearby.   ☐

   You will take the chickens for a walk tomorrow.   ☐

   (1 mark)

5. Circle the incorrect pronoun in each sentence. Then, write the correct pronoun.

   My mother and me saw them at my house.   ....

   Us ate the ramen he couldn't take with him.   ....

   (1 mark)

6. Add a word from the same word family as the words in brackets to complete the sentences below.

The army will .... the enemy to trap them. (*round*)

She wants to .... the garden to build a pool. (*extent*)

In the woods there's a .... where there are no trees. (*clear*)

He read a .... to learn about the singer's life. (*graph*)

(2 marks)

7. Complete the sentences by adding a colon or semicolon and then a second clause.

Maha knew she couldn't win ....

....

Rami dug a hole ....

....

(2 marks)

8. There are six spelling mistakes in the passage below. Rewrite the passage, correcting all of the mistakes.

> I absolutly want to visit the spectacular parliment building while we are here. It is unlikly to be busy and, if we run speedely, we can easly go there before our tour of the Cathlic cathedral.

....

....

....

....

....

(3 marks)

Score: /12

Summer Term: Workout 1

Warm up

1. Underline the preposition in each sentence.

    Secrets lie beneath the murky water's surface.

    The fish live among many mystical creatures.

    (1 mark)

2. In each pair, circle the word that is spelt correctly.

    a) crucial   crutial   b) influencial   influential

    c) artificial   artifitial   d) offitial   official

    (1 mark)

3. Complete the sentences with pronouns that can replace the nouns in brackets.

    I did a lap around the pond and .... (*my friends*) timed how long it took.

    Gia said her kite was torn so .... (*Gia*) tried to repair .... (*the kite*).

    (1 mark)

4. Underline the adverbial phrase in each sentence.

    The runners coped with the rocky terrain surprisingly well.

    In the distance, an enormous grizzly bear appeared.

    (1 mark)

5. Add six missing punctuation marks to complete the bullet point list below.

    My updated bucket list

        abseiling down a rock face in the Peak District

        a trip to Iceland to see a volcano;

        going on a safari with Will and Indiyah

    (2 marks)

6. In each sentence, underline the word that uses an incorrect prefix.
Then, rewrite the word with the correct prefix on the line.

I find it inpolite when people are impatient. ....

Her immaturity made her inresponsible. ....

(1 mark)

7. Rewrite the sentences below so they use formal language.

This algebra is well hard, isn't it?

....

Cheers — I ain't got no more questions.

....

(2 marks)

8. There are six punctuation mistakes in the passage below.
Rewrite the passage with the correct punctuation.

> I'm suffering from a strained vocal cord — Ive developed the problem due to yodelling too much? Doctor musa — my local GP says it isn't serious, but its vital that I drink plenty of water

....

....

....

....

....

(3 marks)

Score: /12

Summer Term: Workout 2

> **Warm up**
>
> 1. In each pair, underline the sentence that includes an adjective.
>
>   a) Amy always spoke very confidently.   They had a leisurely stroll together.
>
>   b) The birds hid from the cold.   Zoe's bubbly personality lit up the room.
>
>   *(1 mark)*
>
> 2. In each sentence, circle the word that has a silent letter.
>
>   We saw the hot-air balloon ascend into the sky.
>
>   The family climbed the hill with grit and determination.
>
>   *(1 mark)*

3. Tick each sentence where the main clause is underlined.

   <u>We are going to look for seashells</u> when the tide goes out. ☐

   Even when it rains and snows, <u>Wren does his paper round</u>. ☐

   Tom can't go to ballet <u>because he has a dental appointment</u>. ☐

   (1 mark)

4. Add three paragraph markers (//) to the passage below.

   Faiza spent the night plotting how to avoid doing her maths test. She thought about it for hours. The next morning, Faiza told her dad that she had 'come down with something'. She performed a few coughs for effect. "Best to be cautious," she croaked, crawling back into bed. "Nice try," he replied. "Now get dressed."

   (1 mark)

5. Complete the sentences by adding a suitable adverb that shows place.

   She looked up at the eagle flying .... her.

   We looked .... for the rare diamonds but could not find them.

   (1 mark)

6. Add semicolons in the correct places in the sentences below.

   When I get home, I need to do my history and maths homework launch a rocket wash the dishes, which are by the sink and call my gran.

   In the antique shop, we found a necklace, which was over one hundred years old a clock that was broken a set of forks and spoons and a very strange key.

   (2 marks)

7. Rewrite the sentences below, adding commas in the correct places.

   My art project uses twigs sand card and glitter.

   ....

   We'll mop sweep the floors hoover and dust.

   ....

   (2 marks)

8. There are six spelling mistakes in the passage below.
   Rewrite the passage, correcting all of the mistakes.

   > Our dogs are the nation's heros, exemplifying freindship and loyalty.
   > So, why not reward that with a personalized edable treat for your pup?
   > Delectable and affordible, they're flying off the shelfs, so get in quick!

   ....

   ....

   ....

   ....

   ....

   (3 marks)

   Score: /12

Summer Term: Workout 3

Warm up

1. Underline the verb in each sentence.

    Take Kara to her saxophone recital tomorrow.

    Akeem busies himself with party preparations.

    (1 mark)

2. In each pair, circle the word with the correct prefix.

    a) inqualified   unqualified   b) mismatch   dismatch

    c) misguided   disguided   d) retached   detached

    (1 mark)

3. Fill in the missing letter or letters to complete each word.

    You forgot the de........imal point.   I need va........ines before my holiday.

    They found a blo........ed drain.   Me........anical issues delayed the flight.

    (1 mark)

4. Tick each sentence that uses dashes correctly.

    Jax is busy tonight — he is going to a silent disco. ☐

    After the carnival — we are eating at a sushi restaurant. ☐

    This beach resort is amazing — I love surfing here! ☐

    (1 mark)

5. Add the missing commas to the passage below.

    After the curtain came down I stole Holly Wood for a chat about her theatre debut. Wood who found fame on the big screen told me she's relishing the change. Provided that all goes well she could become a theatre star too.

    (1 mark)

6. Complete the passage with the simple past form of the verbs in brackets.

The dormouse .... (to sleep) soundly atop a copper bed of leaves.

When I .... (to wake) him, he .... (to stir) for a

second, then .... (to shake) in fright and scurried away from me.

(2 marks)

7. Underline the modal verbs in the sentence below. Then, rewrite the sentence, making it more certain by using different modal verbs.

I might go to choir practice, then Drew could get his work done.

....

....

(2 marks)

8. Rewrite the passage below in the passive voice.

> A girl with a hood spray-painted the wall. Kai watched her every move. Spray paint covered the bricks — paint also splattered the ground. Then, the artist photographed the graffiti. Kai liked the art.

....

....

....

....

....

....

(3 marks)

Score: / 12

Summer Term: Workout 4

Warm up

1. Tick the sentence which uses a comparative.

   Doing a daily crossword has made my brain sharper than it used to be. ☐

   This year, I grew some sunflowers that were the tallest I had ever seen. ☐

   (1 mark)

2. Underline the relative clause in each sentence.

   Music that includes a trombone solo is my favourite.

   Tamara is my younger sister who wants to get married.

   (1 mark)

3. Circle the correct determiner to complete the sentences.

   Bradley wants to have **a / an / the** go at being in goal.

   Layla says pizza is the best thing in **a / an / the** universe.

   I am **a / an / the** amateur photographer in my free time.

   (1 mark)

4. Underline where punctuation has been used incorrectly in the passage below.

   I think edinburgh is great? You can walk everywhere and the buildings are breathtaking. there is also a lot of history to explore in the scottish capital.

   (1 mark)

5. Complete each sentence by replacing the words in brackets with a possessive pronoun.

   Lots of schools make you wear a uniform but .... (*our school*) doesn't.

   This one is my seat but I don't know where .... (*your seat*) is.

   My sister's hair is dark brown but .... (*my hair*) is auburn.

   Jay threw my frisbee into the lake so he gave me .... (*Jay's frisbee*).

   (2 marks)

6. Complete each sentence using the correct form of the word in brackets so that the sentence is written in Standard English.

   Cherish always sings so .... (*nice*).

   We can fix that for you .... (*easy*).

   (1 mark)

7. Complete the words in each sentence with either 'cious' or 'tious'.

   My neighbour's dog can be quite vi............... with cats.

   My brother-in-law's apple pie is absolutely scrump............... .

   The market sells the ripest and most lus............... peaches.

   Santosh is supersti............... about walking under ladders.

   (2 marks)

8. There are six spelling mistakes in the passage below. Rewrite the passage, correcting all of the mistakes.

   I waited for an eternity in the shop que. I'm not exagerating. I can garantee it took hours to be served. The people filed up and down the ailes for miles, and the staff did not comunicate with us. It was extremely awquard.

   ....

   ....

   ....

   ....

   ....

   ....

   (3 marks)

   Score: / 12

Summer Term: Workout 5

Warm up

1. Underline the modal verb in each of the sentences below.

   a) Will Scarlett collect the frogspawn tomorrow?

   b) Aaron should be there to show you around.

   (1 mark)

2. In each pair, circle the word that is spelt correctly.

   a) ancious   anxious   b) contious   conscious

   c) pretentious   pretencious   d) nutritious   nutrixious

   (1 mark)

3. Add a suitable 'ough' word to the gaps to complete each sentence below.

   We were hungry as Rory didn't bring .... rice for everyone.

   Cleo tried to save water due to the .... that summer.

   (1 mark)

4. Tick each sentence where removing the hyphen would change the meaning.

   The brand-new menu featured croissants and other pastries. ☐

   Tomek plans to re-form the local neighbourhood council. ☐

   I bought a little-used sofa on the internet and it arrived yesterday. ☐

   (1 mark)

5. Finish the sentences by adding a conjunction and then a second clause.
   Use different conjunctions for each sentence.

   Iqra dislikes cheese ....

   ....

   We could go to the match now ....

   ....

   (2 marks)

6. Circle the subject and underline the object in each of the sentences below.

   Malachi hugged Declan tightly.   Did Jade print out her work?

   It was Priya I saw on that fateful night.   Al put the plates on the table.

   (2 marks)

7. Add a comma to the second sentence in each pair so that it has the same meaning as the first sentence.

   Kiara had pasta and salad and soup for lunch.

   Kiara had pasta salad and soup for lunch.

   Sasha loves to paint her cat as well as watching films and seeing her friends.

   Sasha loves painting her cat watching films and seeing her friends.

   (1 mark)

8. There are six words in the passage below which use incorrect prefixes. Rewrite the passage, correcting all the mistakes.

   Levi Tate, denatural investigator and ghost expert, is releasing his superbiography. The normally shy and supersocial star gave an exclusive antiview and devealed that a supervisor oversees investigations to ensure no one can refere with any ghostly incidents.

   ....

   ....

   ....

   ....

   ....

   ....

   (3 marks)

   Score: / 12

Summer Term: Workout 6

> **Warm up**
>
> 1. Circle the adverb in each of the sentences below.
>
>   a) The elderly cat dozed lazily on the floor, snoring.
>
>   b) Evan often asked for the orange sweets, but I thought they were ghastly.
>
>   *(1 mark)*
>
> 2. Tick all the words that have had suffixes added correctly.
>
>   amuseing ☐   busily ☐   frenzied ☐
>
>   hungryly ☐   unifyed ☐   nastily ☐
>
>   *(1 mark)*

3. Add the missing dashes to the sentences below.

   Dr Robbins my physics teacher showed us how lasers work.

   Ruby was exhausted she had not managed to sleep at all.

   Everyone except for Margot had brought their scarves.

   (1 mark)

4. Write a suitable determiner next to each sentence that could replace the underlined determiners which have been used incorrectly.

   Don't buy too <u>much</u> snacks for the journey.   ....

   I've only met <u>this</u> of these people before.   ....

   Have you very <u>many</u> experience in this area?   ....

   (1 mark)

5. Add 'in-', 'il-', 'im-' or 'ir-' to each of these words to give them their opposite meaning.

   logical   ....   regular   ....

   mortal   ....   tolerant   ....

   (2 marks)

6. Circle the correct spelling of each word to complete the sentences below.

   The castle was damaged in a **seige** / **siege** hundreds of years ago.

   I thought it was **wierd** / **weird** that he changed his mind at the last minute.

   My **niece** / **neice** had her first birthday at the weekend.

   (1 mark)

7. Underline the noun phrase in each sentence, then expand each noun phrase with adjectives or a preposition phrase on the line below.

   Annabelle received a letter.

   ....

   Harrison left the house.

   ....

   (2 marks)

8. Rewrite the passage below using bullet points.

   Pupils will need to bring the following items for the annual Year 7 camping trip a pillow or two, warm pyjamas and thick socks, a torch (with some spare batteries) and a sleeping bag.

   ....

   ....

   ....

   ....

   ....

   ....

   (3 marks)

   Score: /12

Summer Term: Workout 7

Warm up

1. Underline the conjunction in each of the sentences below.

   Since we're here, we should eat.   It was fun, but now I'm tired.

   (1 mark)

2. Draw lines to show whether the apostrophes show singular or plural possession.

   The flower's petals began to open.

   The tigers' roars rumbled loudly.   singular

   Ross's parcel took a month to arrive.

   plural

   (1 mark)

3. Tick each sentence that uses pronouns correctly.

   Cynthia and Nevaeh forgot their bags, so went back for her.   ☐

   Mason put the pencils back as he knew where they went.   ☐

   Finley admired the painting as he thought they was beautiful.   ☐

   (1 mark)

4. Circle the comma which is used incorrectly in each of the sentences below.

   Yesterday, afternoon, Yaseen found his old games console.
   Very slowly, the sloth, made its way down from the tree.
   Underneath the hedge, the hedgehogs, slept peacefully.

   (1 mark)

5. Write the correct spelling of the words in bold on the lines below.

   Azaan and Cora performed an **elegent** dance.   ....

   Aoife is messing around and being a **nuisence**.   ....

   We only accept shillings as **currancy** at the shop.   ....

   (1 mark)

6. Add the correct word endings to the gaps to complete the words in the sentences below.

   Blood pres............... is how strongly your heart pumps blood around your body.

   The tex............... of the expensive fabric was very soft and smooth.

   While this is a disappointing result, we will try to do better in the fu............... .

   The evil king glowered down at the hero with displea............... .

   (2 marks)

7. Rewrite the sentences below so that the verbs use Standard English.

   They is performing at a concert I am go to.

   ....

   She were quick — Harper had already did it.

   ....

   (2 marks)

8. There are six incorrect words in the passage below. Rewrite the passage, correcting all the mistakes.

   > Safa was feeling board when Monty burst into the room.
   > "Have you scene my leak? I need it for the soup!" Safa gave a grown.
   > "It was all mouldy and vial," she said. "I have throne it in the compost."

   ....

   ....

   ....

   ....

   ....

   (3 marks)

   Score: / 12

Summer Term: Workout 8

Warm up

1. In each sentence, circle the adverb that shows how possible something is.

   a) Maybe next time you won't seriously overcook the pasta.

   b) Aizah is definitely coming to the party, although she'll be late.

   (1 mark)

2. Tick each sentence where the verb agrees with its subject.

   The passengers embark. ☐   Ella roll her eyes. ☐

   The builders repairs the roof. ☐   Imran sweeps the floor. ☐

   (1 mark)

3. Add a suffix to each of the nouns below to make them adjectives.

   danger ....   frill ....

   cuddle ....   rebel ....

   (1 mark)

4. Rewrite the sentence below, adding a dash in the correct place.

   We all jumped in our seats the loud noise caught us by surprise.

   ....

   ....

   (1 mark)

5. For each category, write two conjunctions that show time, place and cause on the lines.

   time ....

   place ....

   cause ....

   (2 marks)

6. Rewrite each verb in the form given in brackets.

   I speak. *(present perfect)* ....

   We perform. *(past perfect)* ....

   (1 mark)

7. Add a prefix to the words below to complete the sentences.

   In the garden, we made a ....markable discovery. We found a note, but ....looked how strange it was. At first, we ....understood the message, because the handwriting ....tracted us. Then, we tried ....reading the note and managed to ....code its secret message.

   (2 marks)

8. Rewrite the passage below, adding three pairs of brackets in the correct places.

   Wear gloves some made from tough material and use a trowel to dig a hole usually twice the depth of the bulb. Make sure the pointy part of the bulb called the 'nose' is pointing upwards and place the bulb in the soil. Then, cover the bulb with soil and sprinkle some water on it.

   ....

   ....

   ....

   ....

   ....

   ....

   ....

   (3 marks)

   Score: /12

Summer Term: Workout 9

Warm up

1. In each pair, circle the word that is spelt correctly.

   a) possible   possable   b) horrable   horrible

   c) inflatible   inflatable   d) adorable   adorible

   (1 mark)

2. In each pair, underline the sentence that uses a preposition.

   a) After a break, she began college.   Each snowflake has a unique pattern.

   b) We no longer collect these items.   I like the restaurant opposite the theatre.

   (1 mark)

3. Add the suffix in the brackets to the word in bold.

   Alexander **prefer** (ed) .... shorter films.

   The runner **suffer** (ed) .... an ankle injury.

   (1 mark)

4. Circle the correct word to complete each sentence below.

   It is **essential / essencial** that you bring a grandfather clock on holiday.

   We asked an accountant for some **finantial / financial** advice.

   He showed me the **confidential / confidencial** documents.

   (1 mark)

5. Add a semicolon in the correct place in each sentence below.

   We could see a play on Saturday you can buy tickets online.

   Antoni wants to go to the museum his sister would rather stay at home.

   Effie entered the crochet competition it takes place next month.

   (1 mark)

6. Underline the modal verbs in the sentence below. Then, rewrite the sentence, making it less certain by using different modal verbs.

   Shazia must be back before midnight as the gates will be locked.

   ....

   ....
   (2 marks)

7. Rewrite the sentences below, adding dashes in the correct places.

   My teacher Mr Brown set us homework.

   ....

   We saw a mandrill a type of monkey on the safari.

   ....

   ....
   (2 marks)

8. Rewrite the passage below so that it is in the simple past tense.

   > My family flies to Italy for a holiday. We all have a great time! We begin our trip in Rome, where I visit the Colosseum and take plenty of pictures. I eat gelato every day of the trip.

   ....

   ....

   ....

   ....
   (3 marks)

   Score: ☐ /12

Summer Term: Workout 10

> **Warm up**
>
> 1. In each pair, underline the sentence that uses a hyphen correctly.
>
>   a) I read a thought-provoking book.   Ravi wants to play video-games.
>
>   b) You added chocolate-chips to the cake.   I had lunch in a dog-friendly cafe.
>
>   *(1 mark)*
>
> 2. In each group of words, circle the word that can have the determiner 'an' before it.
>
>   a) umpire   papaya   newspaper
>
>   b) raccoon   uniform   accordion
>
>   *(1 mark)*

3. Write 'P' if the sentence uses passive voice and 'A' if it uses active voice.

   a) Mo made a carrot cake. ....   b) A jar was opened by Anna. ....

   c) The letters were posted. ....   d) The newt ate some insects. ....

   (1 mark)

4. Circle the comma which is used incorrectly in each of the sentences below.

   Without a sound, the owl flew, over the fields.

   This morning, Sam fell over, and injured his leg.

   Quite, amused, Miranda tried to hide a grin.

   (1 mark)

5. Complete each sentence with an antonym of the word in brackets.

   The information we were given was .... (*essential*)

   The ballet dancers moved in a .... way. (*clumsy*)

   The sorcerer caused the mountain to .... (*vanish*)

   Gooseberries are .... in the summer months. (*scarce*)

   (2 marks)

6. Tick each sentence where the adverbial phrase is underlined.

Lucas looked <u>with desperation</u> for his missing sock. ☐

The detective checked <u>the new evidence</u>. ☐

<u>In the evening</u>, Mei played football outside. ☐

(1 mark)

7. In each sentence, underline the word that is spelt incorrectly.
Then, write the correct spelling of the word on the line.

Charlotte breifly glimpsed a solitary reindeer. ....

The reciept for the jewellery was inaccurate. ....

We stole the dictionary during the librery heist. ....

He shreiked with glee as he entered the gallery. ....

(2 marks)

8. There are six spelling mistakes in the passage below.
Rewrite the passage, correcting all of the mistakes.

> Pasions are running high at this actian-packed hockey competission.
> The Kirkton Koalas have great technik, but the Lowmoss Limes'
> determinasion might win it for them. Who will finish top of the leage?

....

....

....

....

....

(3 marks)

Score: ☐ / 12

Summer Term: Workout 11

> **Warm up**
>
> 1. Underline the word that is spelt incorrectly in each sentence.
>
>   Tegan was heavily involved with her local amature dramatic society.
>
>   Otto felt his stomack start to rumble as he observed the marvellous pastries.
>
>   *(1 mark)*
>
> 2. Circle the abstract noun in each sentence.
>
>   Katie is learning to drive so she can gain some independence.
>
>   He showed great bravery before the surgery on his leg.
>
>   *(1 mark)*

3. Tick each sentence that uses brackets correctly.

   Yusuf brought (Mimi his pet dog) to the park. ☐

   Janey spent her savings (over £200) on a recorder. ☐

   I thought that he (Mia's brother) was being rude. ☐

   (1 mark)

4. Add the suffix to each root word and write the new word on the line.

   plenty + ful   ....

   rare + ity   ....

   admire + ation ....

   (1 mark)

5. Rewrite the sentences so that they are in the past progressive (continuous) form.

   Sara swam all day while Bertie slept.

   ....

   They listened to music as they walked.

   ....

   (2 marks)

6. Use a line (|) to separate the main clause and the subordinate clause in each sentence below.

   I ate some coconut cake while I waited for my fruit salad.

   Although the weather was bad, we all enjoyed the outdoor opera concert.

   Angus will make pancakes for everyone if he can find the milk.
   (1 mark)

7. Add a word from the same word family as the word in brackets to complete the sentence below.

   They will celebrate twenty years of .... next week. *(remarry)*

   We went to the .... to catch a plane. *(port)*

   The .... is in a first aid kit. *(thermal)*

   The play had many .... moments. *(memory)*
   (2 marks)

8. There are six punctuation marks missing from the passage below. Rewrite the passage, adding the missing punctuation.

   > We've been expecting you for some time" the man said. He opened the door its hinges creaking as he did so. He smiled in a way that didnt reach his eyes. "You must follow me," he commanded "as dinner is about to begin"

   ....

   ....

   ....

   ....

   ....
   (3 marks)

   Score: /12

Summer Term: Workout 12

Warm up

1. Circle the relative pronoun in each sentence.

    He played the glockenspiel that his sister gave to him.

    I saw the celebrity whom everyone was talking about.

    (1 mark)

2. Underline the word that has a silent letter in each sentence.

    We'll need to phone a plumber about that octopus in the drains.

    The recipe says to separate the egg yolks and add them slowly.

    (1 mark)

3. Use a suitable co-ordinating conjunction to complete each sentence below.

    Amahle wore her warmest coat .... she would not be cold.

    He didn't cook .... did he help clean up afterwards.

    Swimming improves your fitness .... it is relaxing.

    (1 mark)

4. Underline the word that uses the wrong prefix in each sentence.

    The supersized hailstones disrupted our extranight flight to America.

    Soon we will overhaul our systems and create an antimatic process.

    The doctor prescribed a course of debiotics to treat the symptoms of infection.

    (1 mark)

5. Tick each sentence that uses the subjunctive form.

    Henley demanded that we take a break. ☐

    If it were possible, Soraya would live in space. ☐

    I will not be at the party as I'm going to Leeds. ☐

    (1 mark)

6. Add 'ancy' or 'ency' to complete the words in each sentence below.

   Our teacher announced her pregn............... to the class.

   Christopher has a tend............... to forget he is a goat.

   Let's check if there is a vac............... at the hotel.

   Roisin said the pickle debate was a matter of great urg............... .

   (2 marks)

7. Rewrite the sentences below, adding colons and commas in the correct places.

   I have many hobbies writing cooking and singing.

   ....

   The box contains oranges apples pears and grapes.

   ....

   (2 marks)

8. Rewrite the passage below, replacing the words in bold with synonyms and the underlined words with antonyms.

   > I felt **scared** as I entered the <u>sturdy</u> house. The **weak** candlelight didn't show much and I **shivered** at the thought of what might live inside. I heard a <u>calming</u> noise and turned quickly, which <u>ignited</u> my candle.

   ....

   ....

   ....

   ....

   ....

   ....

   (3 marks)

   Score: ___ / 12

Answers

Autumn Term

Workout 1 — pages 2-3

1. **a)** illegible **b)** improbable
   c) irrelevant **d)** informal
   (1 mark for all 4 correct)

2. Obi was absolutely <u>ravenous</u>.
   Jackie sprinted after the <u>greedy</u> squirrel.
   (1 mark for both correct)

3. The zookeeper tried to make the snake from <u>Z</u>ambia feel comfortable<u>.</u>
   <u>S</u>he fed it plenty of delicious food and gave it a cuddly bear<u>.</u>
   (1 mark for all 4 correct)

4. Abed's mum, who loves football, is a referee.
   The violin, a string instrument, is Bob's favourite.
   (1 mark for both correct)

5. Rajesh, Simon
   (1 mark for both correct)

6. Debbie wanted to show <u>him</u> some videos, but <u>she</u> accidentally deleted <u>them</u>.
   <u>They</u> took the car, parked <u>it</u> at the shop and got <u>me</u> a present.
   (2 marks available — 1 mark for each correct sentence)

7. E.g. Ron wants to ride his bike <u>but</u> it's raining.
   Paula has eaten a pizza <u>and</u> she plans to eat another.
   (2 marks available — 1 mark for each suitable conjunction)

8. Mizuki was <u>grateful</u> that her father had agreed to go skydiving. While Mizuki was <u>fearless</u> and loved scary <u>activities</u>, her father got little <u>enjoyment</u> from them. As the day approached, he looked <u>glummer</u> and more <u>nervous</u>.
   (3 marks available — 1 mark for every 2 words correctly rewritten)

Workout 2 — pages 4-5

1. **a)** primarily **b)** admitted
   c) controlling **d)** miserably
   (1 mark for all 4 correct)

2. We saw a <u>flock</u> of geese raid the corner shop.
   Freya's <u>pack</u> of wolves often roamed at night.
   (1 mark for both correct)

3. The wily <u>foxes</u> were friends with the <u>donkeys</u>.
   They disliked the two <u>wolves</u> who ate their <u>berries</u>.
   (1 mark for all 4 correct)

4. You're the artist who refuses to use the colour purple.
   I bought a hamster that has black and white spots.
   (1 mark for both correct)

5. buys, spoke
   (1 mark for both correct)

6. The tour guide provided little <u>assistance</u>.
   The spider in the bath was an <u>emergency</u>.
   Shanice was a <u>resident</u> at the lighthouse.
   Louisa was a very <u>vigilant</u> security guard.
   (2 marks available — 1 mark for every 2 words correctly underlined)

7. "I enjoyed the sushi," said Lucas.
   The lawyer yelled, "It's him — the clown is guilty!"
   (2 marks available — 1 mark for each correct sentence)

8. Today we <u>are</u> at the beach — I <u>am</u> having a great time! Jeff made sandwiches, Meera <u>has</u> got a beachball and I <u>have</u> brought towels. It is perfect here — the waves <u>roll</u> gently and the sun <u>warms</u> us as we sunbathe.
   (3 marks available — 1 mark for every 2 words correctly rewritten)

Workout 3 — pages 6-7

1. The expensive planes <u>zoomed</u> over our house.
   <u>Borrow</u> the golden lunchbox next week.
   (1 mark for both correct)

2. **a)** difference **b)** factory
   c) enemies **d)** general
   (1 mark for all 4 correct)

3. If you need <u>an</u> umbrella to avoid <u>the</u> rain, there are some in the cupboard.
   I wanted to teach her <u>a</u> lesson about rinsing <u>the</u> dishes.
   (1 mark for all 4 correct)

4. The <u>girl's</u> thought the children's dolls were creepy.
   Chris's niece liked the <u>dress'</u> colour and pattern.
   Both frogs' tadpoles can be found in the <u>mans'</u> pond.
   (1 mark for all 3 correct)

5. Greg <u>replaced</u> his broken spatula with a shiny new one.
   Poppy thought golf was fun but Nina <u>disagreed</u>.
   Grace sped up so she could <u>overtake</u> the pedestrians.
   Tara wanted to empty the freezer and <u>defrost</u> it.
   (2 marks available — 1 mark for every 2 prefixes correctly added)

6. Ricardo crashed his bike <u>on</u> the way home.
   The grey squirrel leapt <u>over</u> my garden fence.
   Tamsin will be riding Lola's horse <u>until</u> sunset.
   (1 mark for all 3 correct)

7. We chased after <u>them</u>.
   <u>They</u> built <u>it</u> at home.
   (2 marks available — 1 mark for each correct sentence)

8. What can you do on a trip to Japan<u>?</u> You can also eat fresh sashimi (a raw fish dish<u>)</u> and take a trip to a <u>t</u>emple in Kyoto. If you enjoy hiking or climbing, there's one place you must go<u>:</u> Mount Fuji<u>.</u> All this and much more awaits.
   (3 marks available — 1 mark for every 2 mistakes corrected)

Workout 4 — pages 8-9

1. **a)** honest **b)** napkin
   c) assign **d)** descend
   (1 mark for all 4 correct)

2. **a)** Frankie's dress sparkled brightly.
   b) His grey cat is very patient.
   (1 mark for both correct)

Answers 74 © CGP — not to be photocopied

Answers

3. You <u>must</u> decide which lorry you wish to drive.
   I want to watch a film, but we <u>could</u> go salsa dancing instead.
   (1 mark for both correct)

4. <u>While I go to the gym</u>, Martha will play the piano.
   Do not open the door <u>until the parrot has been caught</u>.
   (1 mark for both correct)

5. uncontrolled, indirectness, immature
   (1 mark for all 3 correct)

6. Once the turkey is in the oven, we need to boil the carrots, the parsnips and the peas. Later on, we'll need to roast the potatoes, make gravy, get the cutlery from the drawer, set the table and serve drinks.
   (2 marks available — 1 mark for every 3 commas correctly added)

7. I need to <u>re-cover</u> the car before it snows.
   Watch out for the <u>bear-eating</u> fish.
   (2 marks available — 1 mark for each correct sentence)

8. In my favourite game, you are a robot who is <u>disguised</u> as a human and <u>has</u> to learn about Earth. I <u>bought</u> this game years ago, but I <u>lost</u> my copy. However, I <u>met</u> the creator yesterday and he <u>gave</u> me a new one!
   (3 marks available — 1 mark for every 2 words correctly rewritten)

Workout 5 — pages 10-11

1. Today, Connor made <u>some</u> cheese.
   We took home <u>four</u> skunks.
   (1 mark for both correct)

2. a) They won't return the carrots.
   b) Guy said he hadn't eaten.
   (1 mark for both correct)

3. My neighbours — Jen and Marek — like the boats (—) that sail down the river.
   Millie saw (—) the clouds — grey and large — were engulfing the sky.
   Gordon (—) and I made a sandwich — ham and cheese — in the kitchen.
   (1 mark for all 3 correct)

4. I'm going to paint a house today; Nafula will write a poem about dogs.
   We need a few things: a spanner, some nuts and a hammer.
   (1 mark for both correct)

5. mourning — morning
   aloud — allowed
   weather — whether
   brake — break
   (2 marks available — 1 mark for every 2 words correctly underlined and rewritten)

6. That film about cowboys was loads of fun! — informal sentence
   It was an unsavoury end to the evening. — formal sentence
   Ryan may be able to assist you with this. — formal sentence
   I was rubbish and blew it for our team. — informal sentence
   (1 mark for all 4 correct)

7. I am diving into the custard.
   We are travelling to the car wash.
   (2 marks available — 1 mark for each correct sentence)

8. A <u>musician</u> came to our school as a <u>special</u> guest. We had a fascinating <u>discussion</u> about her <u>television</u> appearances. However, I felt <u>frustration</u> when she signed autographs with just her first <u>initial</u> and not her whole name.
   (3 marks available — 1 mark for every 2 words correctly rewritten)

Workout 6 — pages 12-13

1. Naoto <u>carved</u> adorable mice into the celery.
   My chin began to <u>ache</u> after my rugby match.
   (1 mark for both correct)

2. a) The blue football is hers.
   b) I have two, so use mine.
   (1 mark for both correct)

3. On his days off, <u>Riyad gives tours on his fishing boat</u>.
   <u>My cat sleeps</u> for most of the day.
   (1 mark for both correct)

4. photograph, supermarket, international
   (1 mark for all 3 correct)

5. It had been a glorious morning when Marcel and Zelda left to go hiking. They had been in high spirits. // Three hours later, they were cold, wet and fed up. Marcel's feet ached and his hands were completely numb. // "Should we just go home?" he asked. // "No, we're nearly at the top of the hill," Zelda said, "so let's keep at it!"
   (1 mark for all 3 correct)

6. criticise, advertise, intensify, glorify
   (2 marks available — 1 mark for every 2 correct)

7. You will find these things in the attic:
   • a photo album from school;
   • my old Christmas tree;
   • a stamp collection;
   • a vintage television that doesn't work.
   (2 marks available — 1 mark for every 2 correct bullet points. Either commas or semicolons can be used)

8. Last night, <u>Jasper and I</u> watched 'Fairy Hippos 3'. We should <u>have</u> arrived at six, but the bus <u>was</u> late so we had to run <u>quickly</u> to get there. We love <u>those</u> films — we <u>have</u> been to see every one.
   (3 marks available — 1 mark for every 2 examples of non-Standard English replaced with Standard English)

Workout 7 — pages 14-15

1. a) antique   b) rogue
   c) clog   d) unique
   (1 mark for all 4 correct)

2. How peculiar that is! — exclamation
   Stop that albatross at once! — command
   Please watch out for the goat! — command
   What a disgusting pizza it is! — exclamation
   (1 mark for all 4 correct)

© CGP — not to be photocopied

Answers

3. Miguel couldn't find his car | after he left the theme park.
   Although it is difficult, | Parvati enjoys scuba diving.
   We had a picnic | before we went to the seaside.
   (1 mark for all 3 correct)

4. During the day, we'll explore a cave where a troll supposedly lives; climb a tower that was built 300 years ago; and visit a tavern with a cosy fire.
   (1 mark for both correct)

5. Hattie drives the tractor through the barn.
   Under the mattress, I found hundreds of pounds.
   (1 mark for both correct)

6. rec<u>ei</u>ve, s<u>ei</u>ze, bel<u>ie</u>ve, n<u>ei</u>ghbour, sh<u>ie</u>ld, gr<u>ie</u>f
   (2 marks available — 1 mark for every 3 words spelt correctly)

7. The volleyball match was enjoyed by everyone.
   Helena's singing was mocked by the parrot.
   (2 marks available — 1 mark for each correct sentence)

8. Eric went to see a play about a <u>treasure</u> hunter who goes on an <u>adventure</u> to find a <u>valuable</u> sword. He said the lead actor was barely <u>audible</u> and the story didn't <u>capture</u> his attention. It sounds like I <u>probably</u> wouldn't enjoy it.
   (3 marks available — 1 mark for every 2 words correctly rewritten)

Workout 8 — pages 16-17

1. Toby plays the cello <u>while</u> Nayeli sings.
   Wanda took her scooter <u>because</u> the bus was cancelled.
   (1 mark for both correct)

2. a) I can't see — it's too dark.
   b) Dean is hiding — he's upstairs.
   (1 mark for both correct)

3. preferring, reference, differed
   (1 mark for all 3 correct)

4. Kyle's new house was rather <u>spacious</u>.
   I had to be <u>cautious</u> when I approached the snake pit.
   Her lovely laughter was <u>infectious</u>.
   Although it was ugly, the doll was <u>precious</u> to him.
   (2 marks available — 1 mark for every 2 words correctly underlined)

5. We had chocolate, cheesecake and popcorn for dinner.
   It is time to go downstairs and eat, Katy.
   I bought a radish, and some glue for my art project.
   (1 mark for all 3 correct)

6. Gabby has the <u>most modern</u> phone out of us all.
   His jumper is <u>brighter</u> than mine.
   Betty is the <u>laziest</u> dog I know.
   (1 mark for all 3 correct)

7. E.g. Zara hit the ball <u>extremely hard</u>.
   We watched the ballet dancer <u>in amazement</u>.
   (2 marks available — 1 mark for each suitable adverbial phrase)

8. Ryu <u>couldn't</u> believe his ticket was gone. So was <u>Edgar's</u>. <u>Iris's</u> too. <u>He'd</u> had them safe in his pocket, but now <u>they'd</u> vanished. He tried not to think about his two <u>friends'</u> disappointment.
   (3 marks available — 1 mark for every 2 apostrophes added correctly)

Workout 9 — pages 18-19

1. Kim is a talented chef <u>who</u> cooks the best pies.
   The koala climbs up the tree <u>that</u> the bird is in.
   (1 mark for both correct)

2. a) plaid   b) grating
   (1 mark for both correct)

3. There's a monkey with a hat dozing on the roof.
   My racket with green stripes is my lucky charm.
   (1 mark for both correct)

4. The captain said, "Head to that island over there."
   "Casper refuses to fly to Chile!" complained Jasminda.
   (1 mark for all 4 correct)

5. Although it had snowed, we still had to go to school(,) the next day.
   Robert is only packing(,) a jumper, two pairs of trainers and hair gel.
   Inside(,) the tunnel, a lorry was stuck and the cars couldn't get past it.
   (1 mark for all 3 correct)

6. underground — place
   Today — time
   therefore — cause
   (2 marks available — 1 mark for all 3 adverbs correctly underlined, 1 mark for identifying what all 3 adverbs show)

7. Sully has leapt over the puddle.
   You have chosen the purple curtains.
   (2 marks available — 1 mark for each correct sentence)

8. It had been a <u>tough</u> day on the farm. Not only had the <u>plough</u> broken, but the <u>oxen</u> had escaped from their <u>enclosure</u> too. Furthermore, the <u>calves</u> had <u>fought</u> one another all afternoon.
   (3 marks available — 1 mark for every 2 words correctly rewritten)

Workout 10 — pages 20-21

1. a) Maggie, the mechanic, is very kind.
   b) My sweets, that are sour, are cheap.
   (1 mark for both correct)

2. a) antidote   b) autopilot
   c) supersonic   d) interact
   (1 mark for all 4 correct)

3. I am feeling really concerned: Isaac twisted his ankle playing softball.
   The gym is closing: everyone stopped going there because of the bats.
   (1 mark for both correct)

Answers

4. If I were you, I would stay away from the laboratory.
   It is vital that Hamza feed the budgie properly.
   (1 mark for both correct)

5. E.g. We <u>might</u> tour the country in a van.
   They <u>could</u> yodel as part of Jamal's song.
   (1 mark for 2 suitable modal verbs)

6. A very nasty <u>scent</u> was coming from the bin.
   Angela <u>typically</u> dances to music in the morning.
   Hank wanted to paint his bedroom walls <u>beige</u>.
   We had to keep my little brother <u>occupied</u>.
   (2 marks available — 1 mark for every 2 correct)

7. The <u>terrifying</u> television programme was <u>dull</u>.
   Her <u>powerful</u> kick is <u>outstanding</u>.
   (2 marks available — 1 mark for every 2 suitable synonyms)

8. The blizzard chilled the explorers and the wind deafened their dogs. Snow shrouded the path; ice covered the ground. Wendy analysed the compass, but Jed falling over distracted her.
   (3 marks available — 1 mark for every 2 verbs correctly rewritten in the active voice)

Workout 11 — pages 22-23

1. concrete nouns: vehicle, mascot
   abstract nouns: sadness, victory
   (1 mark for all 4 correct)

2. a) sleepiness   b) adoration
   c) amusement   d) quizzed
   (1 mark for all 4 correct)

3. Cameron <u>misregarded</u> my advice to take a detour.
   The robber failed to <u>deable</u> the impressive alarm.
   Ofentse misjudged the challenge, but <u>undercame</u> it anyway.
   (1 mark for all 3 correct)

---

4. It's <u>likely</u> that the tree will fall down in the storm.
   Matteo likes to bake, so he's <u>probably</u> in the kitchen.
   (1 mark for both correct)

5. E.g. Will Thomas see you at the party tonight?
   (1 mark for any suitable question)

6. I was bewitched by the <u>glamourous</u> city life. — glamorous
   He'll <u>simplefy</u> the dance for beginners. — simplify
   The lawyer will <u>advize</u> you how to proceed. — advise
   (2 marks available — 1 mark for all 3 mistakes underlined, 1 mark for all 3 words correctly rewritten)

7. My dog is small <u>but</u> she's stronger than you think.
   The soup was cold <u>so</u> he put it in the microwave.
   (2 marks available — 1 mark for each sentence with a suitable conjunction)

8. My friends — Ellie and Jo — are models. My tickets to their fashion show didn<u>'</u>t arrive, so Jo's parents re<u>-</u>sent them to me. At the show, Ellie and Jo wore many outfits<u>:</u> dresses made from emeralds; some dungarees<u>;</u> and long ball gowns.
   (3 marks available — 1 mark for every 2 punctuation marks correctly added)

Workout 12 — pages 24-25

1. Melokuhle wanted to show <u>us</u> the music shop.
   Jacob has an extra umbrella, so Moesha will borrow <u>his</u>.
   (1 mark for both correct)

2. time — while, until
   place — wherever
   cause — because
   (1 mark for all 4 correct)

3. sapphire, delicious, abandoned
   (1 mark for all 3 correct)

---

4. Bella wanted to go(;) to the desert; Cid insisted on visiting the rainforest.
   The milk(;) in the fridge was smelly; the beef was still fresh.
   Zuri is weary; Mona is feeling wide awake(;) after a good night's sleep.
   (1 mark for all 3 correct)

5. ans<u>w</u>er, crum<u>b</u>, <u>k</u>night, bu<u>t</u>cher, ca<u>l</u>ming, bisc<u>u</u>it
   (2 marks available — 1 mark for every 3 correct silent letters)

6. They <u>asks</u> for pepperoni, but I want pineapple on my pizza.
   Ralph <u>play</u> snooker on Tuesdays and naps when he returns home.
   We are worried about going on the ride because it <u>go</u> very fast.
   (1 mark for all 3 correct)

7. Wilson stole silver<u>,</u> earrings and rings from the shop.
   Jess is now going to cook<u>,</u> Julia.
   (2 marks available — 1 mark for each correct sentence)

8. The <u>existence</u> of aliens has been widely <u>disputed</u>. However, there's some <u>expectancy</u> that we'll <u>eventually</u> discover life forms in space. <u>Currently</u> though, there is no reliable <u>evidence</u> that aliens exist.
   (3 marks available — 1 mark for every 2 words correctly rewritten)

Spring Term

Workout 1 — pages 26-27

1. The invention was of little use to the <u>magicion</u>.
   My <u>obsesion</u> with the new version of the game worried Mike.
   (1 mark for both correct)

2. a) The jeans (the white ones) are gone.
   b) She cooked lunch (for both of them).
   (1 mark for both correct)

© CGP — not to be photocopied

Answers

3. Khalid didn't order the steak — he is vegetarian.
   Let's go to watch the roller derby — it starts at four.
   Agnes was on the news — she saved a swan.
   (1 mark for all 3 correct)

4. E.g. Jenny <u>happily</u> went to the ice-cream parlour.
   Ivan was <u>incredibly</u> sad that his package hadn't arrived.
   Olivia is <u>patiently</u> waiting for the tiger to wake up.
   (1 mark for 3 suitable adverbs)

5. We <u>have held</u> a baby alligator.
   They <u>have fallen</u> off the shelf.
   (1 mark for both correct)

6. E.g. Is the rugby match called off?
   Are Samir and Ayesha staying in tonight?
   (2 marks available — 1 mark for each suitable question)

7. George took some medication to <u>lessen</u> the pain.
   It was <u>plain</u> to see that the ship had left without them.
   Alexis took a big <u>piece</u> of cake to the table.
   The famous singer was the little girl's <u>idol</u>.
   (2 marks available — 1 mark for every 2 correct words)

8. E.g. Justin was <u>really inappropriate</u>.
   I am shocked that he <u>has not</u> apologised to Kurt for <u>throwing</u> his bag into the river. <u>It was uncalled for</u>. If I <u>were</u> him, I would get Kurt a <u>present</u> too.
   (3 marks available — 1 mark for every 2 parts of informal language corrected)

Workout 2 — pages 28-29

1. **a)** cough
   b) thorough
   (1 mark for both correct)

2. modal verbs: will, shall
   adverbs: very, rarely
   (1 mark for all 4 correct)

---

3. That is the gentle rhino <u>whose name I have forgotten</u>.
   Julie wants to buy that guitar <u>which is signed by the rock star</u>.
   We found the last chocolate egg <u>Didier had hidden</u>.
   (1 mark for all 3 correct)

4. Before we catch the train<u>,</u> we need to buy a ticket.
   While Tonya went to find Bongani<u>,</u> I called the lion-tamer.
   Because of the tornado warning<u>,</u> it was advised that we all stay at home.
   (1 mark for all 3 correct)

5. The doctors were trying to find the lollipops.
   I heard Bill was swimming with sharks.
   (1 mark for both correct)

6. To decorate my bedroom, I want<u>:</u>
   • A large, green beanbag<u>;</u>
   • <u>S</u>ome silver photo frames to hang on the wall<u>;</u>
   • <u>A</u> poster of my favourite band<u>.</u>
   (2 marks available — 1 mark for every 3 punctuation marks)

7. E.g. the unusual pink tree with no roots
   my nephew's untidy garage beside his house
   (2 marks available — 1 mark for each suitable noun phrase)

8. I thought I was <u>acquiring</u> a <u>reliable</u> table, but I was incorrect. The top was extremely <u>flexible</u> and the legs <u>collapsed</u> constantly. The company are <u>offering</u> me a refund, but I would have preferred a <u>different</u> table.
   (3 marks available — 1 mark for every 2 words correctly rewritten)

Workout 3 — pages 30-31

1. **a)** plaque   **b)** moustache
   c) chaotic   **d)** critique
   (1 mark for all 4 correct)

---

2. The hot-air balloon ride is <u>the greatest</u> prize in the raffle.
   The tiny mouse was <u>the least intimidating</u> creature Omar had ever seen.
   (1 mark for both correct)

3. recede, misfortune, unnatural
   (1 mark for all 3 correct)

4. Satoshi and I hurried into the secret base.
   Rosa and the spy, Clive, met me in a garden.
   (1 mark for both correct)

5. Klara asked Joy — a builder — to fix the broken chimney.
   I rolled two and six — my favourite numbers — on the dice.
   (1 mark for all 4 correct)

6. bruse — bruise
   lesure — leisure
   perswade — persuade
   (2 marks available — 1 mark for all 3 mistakes underlined, 1 mark for all 3 words correctly rewritten)

7. E.g. The fireworks were set off <u>before the show</u>.
   <u>After the game</u>, Murni was exhausted.
   (2 marks available — 1 mark for each suitable preposition phrase)

8. "I can honestly say<u>,</u>" said Noah, "that this is the hottest I<u>'</u>ve ever been."
   Janine replied, "You're being so dramatic, don't you think<u>?</u>"
   <u>"</u>Can you both stop complaining<u>,</u>" snapped Kamil<u>.</u> "It's getting on my nerves."
   (3 marks available — 1 mark for every 2 punctuation marks added correctly)

Workout 4 — pages 32-33

1. The scientists have discovered <u>a new element</u>.
   The sneaky rabbit hides <u>the phone</u>.
   (1 mark for both correct)

2. **a)** measure   **b)** teacher
   c) fracture   **d)** composure
   (1 mark for all 4 correct)

Answers

3. Even though Andi was hungry, she shared half of her crisps.
    Jonny hates early starts, yet he got up at 5 am to catch a flight.
    (1 mark for both correct)

4. Meg will get a taxi home; Pedro plans to use an electric scooter.
    The swimming pool was packed; the golf course was empty.
    (1 mark for both correct)

5. Jimmy and Nora went to the cafe so they could both eat.
    The group was upset that the owner asked them to leave.
    I took Spot to the park and she chased me around.
    The woman offered to help me when she saw I was lost.
    (2 marks available — 1 mark for every 2 correct words)

6. women, quizzes, geese, discos
    (1 mark for all 4 correct)

7. E.g. The disgusting pasta was unpleasant to eat.
    My hard pillow's pattern is very ugly.
    (2 marks available — 1 mark for every 2 suitable antonyms)

8. Rafiq finally arrived in the stadium. He quickly found his seat as the players appeared. // On the pitch, Trudy, Rafiq's partner, waved. She always waved to him before kick-off. // "Go on, Trudy!" yelled Rafiq as the game began.
    (3 marks available — 1 mark for 2 correct paragraphs or 2 marks for all 3 correct paragraphs, and 1 mark for all paragraphs in the correct order)

Workout 5 — pages 34-35

1. a) chords   b) cylinder
    c) percent d) obscure
    (1 mark for all 4 correct)

2. A full moon occurs when the Earth is between the Sun and the Moon.
    I told you about the wet floor earlier and you still slipped.
    (1 mark for all 4 correct)

3. potential, provincial, official, torrential
    (1 mark for all 4 correct)

4. While I waited for the bus, I sent Trevor a text.
    Mila brought the raisins that we needed for the cake.
    (1 mark for both correct)

5. E.g. "Where are the scissors kept?" asked Ching-He.
    "I put the biscuits in the tin," said Anita.
    (2 marks available — 1 mark for each correct sentence)

6. E.g. Paige has no more satsumas because she ate them all.
    The book had a sad ending but we liked it anyway.
    (1 mark for 2 suitable conjunctions)

7. Is this a party for ninety-eight-year-olds?
    A fast-acting teacher saved the day.
    (2 marks available — 1 mark for each correct sentence)

8. Enoki Cafe's menu will warm you up: there's soup served with our bread (it's award-winning!); roast dinners with all the trimmings; jacket potatoes with a hot filling of your choice; various side dishes; and a selection of drinks.
    (3 marks available — 1 mark for every 2 punctuation marks added correctly)

Workout 6 — pages 36-37

1. When she is on holiday, Aliyah takes lots of photographs.
    (1 mark)

2. Felicity often went for a walk in the park.
    Callum felt the yoga class wasn't going well.
    (1 mark for both correct)

3. If you're finding it to be a challenge, the best person to ask is Arjun. He is an excellent source of information.
    (1 mark for all 3 correct)

4. That is some very expensive jewellery.
    I definitely left the keys on the table.
    Did you chop the vegetables?
    (1 mark for all 3 correct)

5. eat, broke
    (1 mark for both correct)

6. Jake had a problem: he did not know what he needed to do.
    Aarav was terrified: he'd just seen a gigantic spider.
    I have holiday plans: I will visit France and Belgium.
    There are two kinds of tree: deciduous and coniferous.
    (2 marks available — 1 mark for every 2 colons added correctly)

7. E.g. It was very careless of you to drop the plates.
    This multi-purpose tool will be very useful.
    The cat's laziness meant she didn't play with toys.
    I have sent you an invitation to my party.
    (2 marks available — 1 mark for every 2 suitable suffixes)

8. Gwen is an ambitious writer. She wrote a glorious story about meeting a ferocious crocodile — it sounded very perilous. I'm suspicious when she says it's entirely fictional as she is always doing outrageous things.
    (3 marks available — 1 mark for every 2 correct spellings)

Workout 7 — pages 38-39

1. a) We sent a postcard from Copenhagen.
    b) There is a family of monsters living under my bed.
    (1 mark for both correct)

2. a) freight   b) address
    c) crescent   d) reign
    (1 mark for all 4 correct)

3. Leo will make a meal from noodles, chicken, onion and peppers.
    (1 mark for all correct punctuation)

4. It was clear what had happened.
    (1 mark)

5. relief, ceiling, fierce
    (1 mark for all 3 correct)

Answers

6. The Isle of Man, located in the Irish Sea, is a beautiful place.
   The coin, which was later confirmed to be ancient, was found here.
   Arthur, my second cousin once removed, turns three today.
   Dr Sato, a respected astronomer, announced her new discovery.
   (2 marks available — 1 mark for every 2 sentences correctly punctuated)

7. tung — tongue
   bouteek — boutique
   mosk — mosque
   fatige — fatigue
   (2 marks available — 1 mark for every 2 words correctly underlined and rewritten)

8. There's a dance competition that my friend Caitlin and I are planning to enter. She's really good, so I'm glad we're performing together. The competition isn't until August, so we've got plenty of time to practise.
   (3 marks available — 1 mark for every 2 correct contractions)

Workout 8 — pages 40-41

1. a) unravel   b) unclean
   c) unknown   d) unequal
   (1 mark for all 4 correct)

2. The squirrel scampered away very quickly.
   There was water covering the sand as far as the eye could see.
   (1 mark for both correct)

3. Eat your lunch | before it gets cold.
   We're going to be late | unless we hurry up.
   You can watch the film | after you finish your geography homework.
   (1 mark for all 3 correct)

4. We bought some brown paper, string, sticky tape, envelopes and a card.
   The nature reserve is home to puffins, barn owls and gannets.
   (1 mark for both correct)

5.
Root word	-ed	-ing
knit	knitted	knitting
decide	decided	deciding
query	queried	querying

   (2 marks available — 1 mark for every 3 correct spellings)

6. There goes the monkey that stole my bread.
   Denis is the person who is training to be a plumber.
   He spoke to the man whose car had been stolen.
   (1 mark for all 3 correct)

7. It was busy when I collected the tickets.
   Ice forms when water freezes.
   We sat and thought about what to do next.
   The cup in the sink has broken.
   (2 marks available — 1 mark for every 2 correct verbs)

8. The magician brought out a box from behind a curtain and stepped inside with a sense of mystery. After roughly ten seconds, he was gone! I was intrigued since there was no explanation for this incredible illusion.
   (3 marks available — 1 mark for every 2 correct spellings)

Workout 9 — pages 42-43

1. a) classify   b) expertise
   c) intensify   d) theorise
   (1 mark for all 4 correct)

2. a) Eddie's rusty unicycle
   b) the odd lorry with the purple lights
   (1 mark for both correct)

3. I hadn't been to the museum since I was a child.
   Denise practised her oboe before the concert began.
   (1 mark for both correct)

4. E.g. I am going to see many hippos at the zoo.
   They searched for that comic in the living room.
   (1 mark for 2 suitable determiners)

5. At the shop, we bought a lemon(,) jelly and baklava.
   Before painting(,) Hiromi, Lee and Tori got the brushes out.
   Kabir, an explorer, sprinted after the robber(,) holding his sack of gems.
   (1 mark for all 3 correct)

6. I shall bring batteries and Marie will find a screwdriver.
   E.g. I might bring batteries and Marie may find a screwdriver.
   (2 marks available — 1 mark for both modal verbs underlined, 1 mark for 2 less certain modal verbs)

7. Dustin and Shani (a teacher) play baseball.
   The pie was fresh (it was made that morning).
   (2 marks available — 1 mark for each correct sentence)

8. Caleb claimed that he was psychic, but I was doubtful. He wrinkled his brow and told me a ghastly spirit was searching for me. I stopped listening, but Caleb has a knack for making me worry...
   (3 marks available — 1 mark for every 2 correct)

Workout 10 — pages 44-45

1. He is taking Daphne and a troupe of performers to Zimbabwe.
   Warmth finally arrives in Cambridge around May, I have found.
   (1 mark for all 4 correct)

2. The men's suits are not stylish.
   Otis's surfboard snapped in half.
   (1 mark for both correct)

3. As a result of the strike, no helmets will be made in the factory.
   Dani wants to swim to the island even though it is far away.
   Robin will visit the historic site where the famous battle took place.
   (1 mark for all 3 correct)

4. command, exclamation, statement
   (1 mark for all 3 correct)

Answers

5. The crow was very clever — it distracted the man and (—) stole his bagel.
   The biscuits (—) Pippa brought were vile — they tasted incredibly salty.
   My uncle loves visiting — he plays (—) in the garden with our dog.
   (1 mark for all 3 correct)

6. occa<u>ssion</u>, politi<u>cian</u>, percu<u>ssion</u>, fic<u>tion</u>, se<u>ssion</u>, fric<u>tion</u>
   (2 marks available — 1 mark for every 3 correct)

7. There was a <u>reasonable</u> growth in <u>attendance</u> today.
   His performance was <u>believable</u> and <u>confident</u>.
   (2 marks available — 1 mark for each sentence correctly rewritten)

8. Karim <u>went</u> to the book signing in London and <u>spoke</u> to his fans. He <u>had</u> a great time until one couple <u>asked</u> him for a picture. He <u>got</u> up to join them, but accidentally <u>spilt</u> his coffee all over himself.
   (3 marks available — 1 mark for every 2 verbs in the simple past tense)

Workout 11 — pages 46-47

1. possessive pronouns: theirs, ours
   relative pronouns: who, which
   (1 mark for all 4 correct)

2. **a)** hideous **b)** furious
   c) humorous **d)** courageous
   (1 mark for all 4 correct)

3. She told me her <u>preference</u> of pie filling.
   Femi was <u>referring</u> to the wrong theme park timetable.
   The video <u>buffered</u> for what seemed like an eternity.
   The <u>referee</u> was annoyed at the crowd yelling at her.
   (2 marks available — 1 mark for every 2 correct)

4. This movie is <u>less interesting</u> than the one about cyclones.
   Robyn sat in the <u>least comfortable</u> chair in the house.
   Their team did <u>worse</u> on the quiz.
   (1 mark for all 3 correct)

5. If I <u>were</u> an engineer, I would create a mechanical dog.
   It is important that he <u>keep</u> the front door shut.
   (1 mark for both correct)

6. My younger brother heard about <u>that girl with the terrific tennis serve</u>.
   <u>Some really annoying dogs</u> keep stealing my sausage rolls.
   <u>His aunty's massive model train set</u> won praise from fellow enthusiasts.
   (1 mark for all 3 correct)

7. E.g. The werewolf howled <u>at the moon</u>.
   Joseph climbed the tree <u>in the park</u>.
   (2 marks available — 1 mark for each suitable preposition phrase)

8. What a bizarre day that was<u>!</u> On my way to town<u>,</u> a car crashed into a pet shop. There were animals everywhere: two dogs, both greyhounds<u>,</u> sprinted away; a flock of budgies took flight<u>;</u> and a cat sauntered off<u>.</u> Do you think they will all be found<u>?</u>
   (3 marks available — 1 mark for every 2 punctuation marks correctly added)

Workout 12 — pages 48-49

1. My friends, an astronaut and an estate agent, both love(,) large spaces.
   The two parrots, which have green feathers(,) and red beaks, are from Africa.
   (1 mark for both correct)

2. **a)** While it's raining, let's make pancakes.
   b) Fay will sleep if we sing softly.
   (1 mark for both correct)

3. realisation, timeliness, homeless
   (1 mark for all 3 correct)

4. The train is due to arrive late.
   You will take the chickens for a walk tomorrow.
   (1 mark for both correct)

5. me — I
   Us — We
   (1 mark for both correct)

6. The army will <u>surround</u> the enemy to trap them.
   She wants to <u>extend</u> the garden to build a pool.
   In the woods there's a <u>clearing</u> where there are no trees.
   He read a <u>biography</u> to learn about the singer's life.
   (2 marks available — 1 mark for every 2 correct words)

7. E.g. Maha knew she couldn't win<u>; time was almost up</u>.
   Rami dug a hole<u>; Roberta filled it with jelly</u>.
   (2 marks available — 1 mark for each suitable clause)

8. I <u>absolutely</u> want to visit the spectacular <u>parliament</u> building while we are here. It is <u>unlikely</u> to be busy and, if we run <u>speedily</u>, we can <u>easily</u> go there before our tour of the <u>Catholic</u> cathedral.
   (3 marks available — 1 mark for every 2 correct words)

Summer Term

Workout 1 — pages 50-51

1. Secrets lie <u>beneath</u> the murky water's surface.
   The fish live <u>among</u> many mystical creatures.
   (1 mark for both correct)

2. **a)** crucial **b)** influential
   c) artificial **d)** official
   (1 mark for all 4 correct)

3. I did a lap around the pond and <u>they</u> timed how long it took.
   Gia said her kite was torn so <u>she</u> tried to repair <u>it</u>.
   (1 mark for all 3 correct)

4. The runners coped with the rocky terrain <u>surprisingly well</u>.
   <u>In the distance</u>, an enormous grizzly bear appeared.
   (1 mark for both correct)

Answers

5. My updated bucket list:
    • abseiling down a rock face in the Peak District;
    • a trip to Iceland to see a volcano;
    • going on a safari with Will and Indiyah.
    (2 marks available — 1 mark for every 3 punctuation marks)

6. inpolite — impolite
    inresponsible — irresponsible
    (1 mark for both correct)

7. Isn't this algebra very hard?
    Thank you — I have not got any more questions.
    (2 marks available — 1 mark for each correct sentence)

8. I'm suffering from a strained vocal cord — I've developed the problem due to yodelling too much. Doctor Musa — my local GP — says it isn't serious, but it's vital that I drink plenty of water.
    (3 marks available — 1 mark for every 2 mistakes corrected)

Workout 2 — pages 52-53

1. a) They had a <u>leisurely</u> stroll together.
    b) Zoe's <u>bubbly</u> personality lit up the room.
    (1 mark for both correct)

2. We saw the hot-air balloon <u>ascend</u> into the sky.
    The family <u>climbed</u> the hill with grit and determination.
    (1 mark for both correct)

3. We are going to look for seashells when the tide goes out.
    Even when it rains and snows, Wren does his paper round.
    (1 mark for both correct)

4. Faiza spent the night plotting how to avoid doing her maths test. She thought about it for hours. // The next morning, Faiza told her dad that she had 'come down with something'. She performed a few coughs for effect. // "Best to be cautious," she croaked, crawling back into bed. // "Nice try," he replied. "Now get dressed."
    (1 mark for all 3 correct)

5. E.g. She looked up at the eagle flying <u>above</u> her.
    We looked <u>everywhere</u> for the rare diamonds but could not find them.
    (1 mark for 2 suitable adverbs)

6. When I get home, I need to do my history and maths homework; launch a rocket; wash the dishes, which are by the sink; and call my gran.
    In the antique shop, we found a necklace, which was over one hundred years old; a clock that was broken; a set of forks and spoons; and a very strange key.
    (2 marks available — 1 mark for every 3 correct semicolons)

7. My art project uses twigs, sand, card and glitter.
    We'll mop, sweep the floors, hoover and dust.
    (2 marks available — 1 mark for each correct sentence)

8. Our dogs are the nation's <u>heroes</u>, exemplifying <u>friendship</u> and loyalty. So, why not reward that with a <u>personalised</u> <u>edible</u> treat for your pup? Delectable and <u>affordable</u>, they're flying off the <u>shelves</u>, so get in quick!
    (3 marks available — 1 mark for every 2 words correctly rewritten)

Workout 3 — pages 54-55

1. <u>Take</u> Kara to her saxophone recital tomorrow.
    Akeem <u>busies</u> himself with party preparations.
    (1 mark for both correct)

2. a) unqualified   b) mismatch
    c) misguided   d) detached
    (1 mark for all 4 correct)

3. You forgot the de<u>c</u>imal point.
    I need va<u>cc</u>ines before my holiday.
    They found a blo<u>ck</u>ed drain.
    Me<u>ch</u>anical issues delayed the flight.
    (1 mark for all 4 correct)

4. Jax is busy tonight — he is going to a silent disco.
    This beach resort is amazing — I love surfing here!
    (1 mark for both correct)

5. After the curtain came down, I stole Holly Wood for a chat about her theatre debut. Wood, who found fame on the big screen, told me she's relishing the change. Provided that all goes well, she could become a theatre star too.
    (1 mark for all 4 correct)

6. The dormouse <u>slept</u> soundly atop a copper bed of leaves. When I <u>woke</u> him, he <u>stirred</u> for a second, then <u>shook</u> in fright and scurried away from me.
    (2 marks available — 1 mark for every 2 verbs in the simple past tense)

7. I <u>might</u> go to choir practice, then Drew <u>could</u> get his work done.
    E.g. I <u>should</u> go to choir practice, then Drew <u>will</u> get his work done.
    (2 marks available — 1 mark for both modal verbs underlined, 1 mark for 2 more certain modal verbs)

8. The wall was spray-painted by a girl with a hood. Her every move was watched by Kai. The bricks were covered by spray paint — the ground was also splattered with paint. Then, the graffiti was photographed by the artist. The art was liked by Kai.
    (3 marks available — 1 mark for every 2 verbs correctly rewritten in the passive voice)

Workout 4 — pages 56-57

1. Doing a daily crossword has made my brain sharper than it used to be.
    (1 mark)

Answers

2. Music <u>that includes a trombone solo</u> is my favourite.
   Tamara is my younger sister <u>who wants to get married</u>.
   (1 mark for both correct)

3. Bradley wants to have <u>a</u> go at being in goal.
   Layla says pizza is the best thing in <u>the</u> universe.
   I am <u>an</u> amateur photographer in my free time.
   (1 mark for all 3 correct)

4. I think <u>e</u>dinburgh is great<u>?</u> You can walk everywhere and the buildings are breathtaking. <u>t</u>here is also a lot of history to explore in the <u>s</u>cottish capital.
   (1 mark for all 4 correct)

5. Lots of schools make you wear a uniform but <u>ours</u> doesn't.
   This one is my seat but I don't know where <u>yours</u> is.
   My sister's hair is dark brown but <u>mine</u> is auburn.
   Jay threw my frisbee into the lake so he gave me <u>his</u>.
   (2 marks available — 1 mark for every 2 correct pronouns)

6. Cherish always sings so <u>nicely</u>.
   We can fix that for you <u>easily</u>.
   (1 mark for both correct)

7. My neighbour's dog can be quite vi<u>cious</u> with cats.
   My brother-in-law's apple pie is absolutely scrump<u>tious</u>.
   The market sells the ripest and most lus<u>cious</u> peaches.
   Santosh is supersti<u>tious</u> about walking under ladders.
   (2 marks available — 1 mark for every 2 correct words)

8. I waited for an eternity in the shop <u>queue</u>. I'm not <u>exaggerating</u>. I can <u>guarantee</u> it took hours to be served. The people filed up and down the <u>aisles</u> for miles, and the staff did not <u>communicate</u> with us. It was extremely <u>awkward</u>.
   (3 marks available — 1 mark for every 2 words correctly rewritten)

Workout 5 — pages 58-59

1. a) <u>Will</u> Scarlett collect the frogspawn tomorrow?
   b) Aaron <u>should</u> be there to show you around.
   (1 mark for both correct)

2. a) anxious   b) conscious
   c) pretentious   d) nutritious
   (1 mark for all 4 correct)

3. We were hungry as Rory didn't bring <u>enough</u> rice for everyone.
   Cleo tried to save water due to the <u>drought</u> that summer.
   (1 mark for both correct)

4. Tomek plans to re-form the local neighbourhood council.
   I bought a little-used sofa on the internet and it arrived yesterday.
   (1 mark for both correct)

5. E.g. Iqra dislikes cheese, <u>but Sarah's favourite food is cheddar</u>.
   We could go to the match now, <u>or we could clean the house</u>.
   (2 marks available — 1 mark for each suitable conjunction and clause)

6. You should have circled:
   Malachi, Jade, I, Al
   You should have underlined:
   Declan, her work, Priya, the plates
   (2 marks available — 1 mark for all subjects circled and 1 mark for all objects underlined)

7. Kiara had pasta<u>,</u> salad and soup for lunch.
   Sasha loves painting her cat<u>,</u> watching films and seeing her friends.
   (1 mark for both correct commas)

8. Levi Tate, <u>super</u>natural investigator and ghost expert, is releasing his <u>auto</u>biography. The normally shy and <u>anti</u>social star gave an exclusive <u>inter</u>view and <u>re</u>vealed that a supervisor oversees investigations to ensure no one can <u>inter</u>fere with any ghostly incidents.
   (3 marks available — 1 mark for every 2 words correctly rewritten)

Workout 6 — pages 60-61

1. a) The elderly cat dozed <u>lazily</u> on the floor, snoring.
   b) Evan <u>often</u> asked for the orange sweets, but I thought they were ghastly.
   (1 mark for both correct)

2. busily, frenzied, nastily
   (1 mark for all 3 correct)

3. Dr Robbins — my physics teacher — showed us how lasers work.
   Ruby was exhausted — she had not managed to sleep at all.
   Everyone — except for Margot — had brought their scarves.
   (1 mark for all correct)

4. E.g. many, some, much
   (1 mark for 3 suitable determiners)

5. <u>il</u>logical, <u>ir</u>regular, <u>im</u>mortal, <u>in</u>tolerant
   (2 marks available — 1 mark for every 2 correct answers)

6. The castle was damaged in a <u>siege</u> hundreds of years ago.
   I thought it was <u>weird</u> that he changed his mind at the last minute.
   My <u>niece</u> had her first birthday at the weekend.
   (1 mark for all 3 correct)

7. E.g. Annabelle received <u>a letter from her friend</u>.
   Harrison left <u>the spooky house in the woods</u>.
   (2 marks available — 1 mark for underlining both noun phrases, 1 mark for expanding both phrases)

8. Pupils will need to bring the following items for the annual Year 7 camping trip:
   • a pillow or two,
   • warm pyjamas and thick socks,
   • a torch (with some spare batteries),
   • a sleeping bag.
   (3 marks available — 1 mark for every 2 bullet points added correctly, 1 mark for correct punctuation. Either commas or semicolons can be used)

© CGP — not to be photocopied

83

Answers

Answers

Workout 7 — pages 62-63

1. a) <u>Since</u> we're here, we should eat.
   b) It was fun, <u>but</u> now I'm tired.
   (1 mark for both correct)

2. singular:
   The flower's petals began to open.
   Ross's parcel took a month to arrive.
   plural:
   The tigers' roars rumbled loudly.
   (1 mark for all 3 correct)

3. Mason put the pencils back as he knew where they went.
   (1 mark)

4. Yesterday(,) afternoon, Yaseen found his old games console.
   Very slowly, the sloth(,) made its way down from the tree.
   Underneath the hedge, the hedgehogs(,) slept peacefully.
   (1 mark for all 3 correct)

5. elegant, nuisance, currency
   (1 mark for all 3 correct)

6. Blood pre<u>ss</u>ure is how strongly your heart pumps blood around your body.
   The tex<u>t</u>ure of the expensive fabric was very soft and smooth.
   While this is a disappointing result, we will try to do better in the fu<u>t</u>ure.
   The evil king glowered down at the hero with displea<u>s</u>ure.
   (2 marks available — 1 mark for every 2 correct answers)

7. They <u>are</u> performing at a concert I am <u>going</u> to.
   She <u>was</u> quick — Harper had already <u>done</u> it.
   (2 marks available — 1 mark for each correct sentence)

8. Safa was feeling <u>bored</u> when Monty burst into the room.
   "Have you <u>seen</u> my <u>leek</u>? I need it for the soup!" Safa gave a <u>groan</u>.
   "It was all mouldy and <u>vile</u>," she said. "I have <u>thrown</u> it in the compost."
   (3 marks available — 1 mark for every 2 words correctly rewritten)

Workout 8 — pages 64-65

1. a) <u>Maybe</u> next time you won't seriously overcook the pasta.
   b) Aizah is <u>definitely</u> coming to the party, although she'll be late.
   (1 mark for both correct)

2. The passengers embark.
   Imran sweeps the floor.
   (1 mark for both correct)

3. dangerous, frilly, cuddly, rebellious
   (1 mark for all 4 correct)

4. We all jumped in our seats — the loud noise caught us by surprise.
   (1 mark)

5. E.g. time — until, once
   place — where, wherever
   cause — because, so
   (2 marks available — 1 mark for every 3 correct conjunctions)

6. I have spoken.
   We had performed.
   (1 mark for both correct)

7. In the garden, we made a <u>remarkable</u> discovery. We found a note, but <u>over</u>looked how strange it was. At first, we <u>mis</u>understood the message, because the handwriting <u>dis</u>tracted us. Then, we tried <u>re</u>reading the note and managed to <u>de</u>code its secret message.
   (2 marks available — 1 mark for every 3 prefixes correctly added)

8. Wear gloves (some made from tough material) and use a trowel to dig a hole (usually twice the depth of the bulb). Make sure the pointy part of the bulb (called the 'nose') is pointing upwards and place the bulb in the soil. Then, cover the bulb with soil and sprinkle some water on it.
   (3 marks available — 1 mark for each pair of brackets correctly placed)

Workout 9 — pages 66-67

1. a) possible   b) horrible
   c) inflatable d) adorable
   (1 mark for all 4 correct)

2. a) After a break, she began college.
   b) I like the restaurant opposite the theatre.
   (1 mark for both correct)

3. Alexander <u>preferred</u> shorter films.
   The runner <u>suffered</u> an ankle injury.
   (1 mark for both correct)

4. It is <u>essential</u> that you bring a grandfather clock on holiday.
   We asked an accountant for some <u>financial</u> advice.
   He showed me the <u>confidential</u> documents.
   (1 mark for all 3 correct)

5. We could see a play on Saturday<u>;</u> you can buy tickets online.
   Antoni wants to go to the museum<u>;</u> his sister would rather stay at home.
   Effie entered the crochet competition<u>;</u> it takes place next month.
   (1 mark for all 3 correct)

6. Shazia <u>must</u> be back before midnight as the gates <u>will</u> be locked.
   E.g. Shazia <u>could</u> be back before midnight as the gates <u>may</u> be locked.
   (2 marks available — 1 mark for underlining the modal verbs, 1 mark for 2 less certain modal verbs)

7. My teacher <u>—</u> Mr Brown <u>—</u> set us homework.
   We saw a mandrill <u>—</u> a type of monkey <u>—</u> on the safari.
   (2 marks available — 1 mark for each pair of dashes placed correctly)

8. My family <u>flew</u> to Italy for a holiday. We all <u>had</u> a great time! We <u>began</u> our trip in Rome, where I <u>visited</u> the Colosseum and <u>took</u> plenty of pictures. I <u>ate</u> gelato every day of the trip.
   (3 marks available — 1 mark for every 2 verbs correctly rewritten)

Workout 10 — pages 68-69

1. a) I read a thought-provoking book.
   b) I had lunch in a dog-friendly cafe.
   (1 mark for both correct)

2. a) umpire   b) accordion
   (1 mark for both correct)

Answers

3. **a)** A   **b)** P
   c) P   **d)** A
   (1 mark for all 4 correct)

4. Without a sound, the owl flew(,) over the fields.
   This morning, Sam fell over(,) and injured his leg.
   Quite(,) amused, Miranda tried to hide a grin.
   (1 mark for all 3 correct)

5. E.g. The information we were given was <u>unnecessary</u>.
   The ballet dancers moved in a <u>graceful</u> way.
   The sorcerer caused the mountain to <u>appear</u>.
   Gooseberries are <u>abundant</u> in the summer months.
   (2 marks available — 1 mark for every 2 suitable antonyms)

6. Lucas looked <u>with desperation</u> for his missing sock.
   <u>In the evening</u>, Mei played football outside.
   (1 mark for both correct)

7. breifly — briefly
   reciept — receipt
   librery — library
   shreiked — shrieked
   (2 marks available — 1 mark for every 2 words correctly underlined and rewritten)

8. <u>Passions</u> are running high at this <u>action</u>-packed hockey <u>competition</u>. The Kirkton Koalas have great <u>technique</u>, but the Lowmoss Limes' <u>determination</u> might win it for them. Who will finish top of the <u>league</u>?
   (3 marks available — 1 mark for every 2 correct spellings)

Workout 11 — pages 70-71

1. Tegan was heavily involved with her local <u>amature</u> dramatic society.
   Otto felt his <u>stomack</u> start to rumble as he observed the marvellous pastries.
   (1 mark for both correct)

2. Katie is learning to drive so she can gain some <u>independence</u>.
   He showed great <u>bravery</u> before the surgery on his leg.
   (1 mark for both correct)

3. Janey spent her savings (over £200) on a recorder.
   I thought that he (Mia's brother) was being rude.
   (1 mark for both correct)

4. plentiful, rarity, admiration
   (1 mark for all 3 correct)

5. Sara <u>was swimming</u> all day while Bertie <u>was sleeping</u>.
   They <u>were listening</u> to music as they <u>were walking</u>.
   (2 marks available — 1 mark for each correct sentence)

6. I ate some coconut cake | while I waited for my fruit salad.
   Although the weather was bad, | we all enjoyed the outdoor opera concert.
   Angus will make pancakes for everyone | if he can find the milk.
   (1 mark for all 3 correct)

7. They will celebrate twenty years of <u>marriage</u> next week.
   We went to the <u>airport</u> to catch a plane.
   The <u>thermometer</u> is in a first aid kit.
   The play had many <u>memorable</u> moments.
   (2 marks available — 1 mark for every 2 correct words)

8. "We've been expecting you for some time_," the man said. He opened the door_, its hinges creaking as he did so. He smiled in a way that didn_,'t reach his eyes. "You must follow me," he commanded_, "as dinner is about to begin._"
   (3 marks available — 1 mark for every 2 correct punctuation marks)

Workout 12 — pages 72-73

1. He played the glockenspiel <u>that</u> his sister gave to him.
   I saw the celebrity <u>whom</u> everyone was talking about.
   (1 mark for both correct)

2. We'll need to phone a <u>plumber</u> about that octopus in the drains.
   The recipe says to separate the egg <u>yolks</u> and add them slowly.
   (1 mark for both correct)

3. E.g. Amahle wore her warmest coat <u>so</u> she would not be cold.
   He didn't cook <u>nor</u> did he help clean up afterwards.
   Swimming improves your fitness <u>and</u> it is relaxing.
   (1 mark for all 3 correct)

4. The supersized hailstones disrupted our <u>extranight</u> flight to America.
   Soon we will overhaul our systems and create an <u>antimatic</u> process.
   The doctor prescribed a course of <u>debiotics</u> to treat the symptoms of infection.
   (1 mark for all 3 correct)

5. Henley demanded that we take a break.
   If it were possible, Soraya would live in space.
   (1 mark for both correct)

6. Our teacher announced her <u>pregnancy</u> to the class.
   Christopher has a <u>tendency</u> to forget he is a goat.
   Let's check if there is a <u>vacancy</u> at the hotel.
   Roisin said the pickle debate was a matter of great <u>urgency</u>.
   (2 marks available — 1 mark for every 2 words circled correctly)

7. I have many hobbies<u>:</u> writing<u>,</u> cooking and singing.
   The box contains<u>:</u> oranges<u>,</u> apples<u>,</u> pears and grapes.
   (2 marks available — 1 mark for both correct colons, 1 mark for all correct commas)

8. E.g. I felt <u>terrified</u> as I entered the <u>derelict</u> house. The <u>faint</u> candlelight didn't show much, and I <u>trembled</u> at the thought of what might live inside. I heard a <u>worrying</u> noise and turned quickly, which <u>extinguished</u> my candle.
   (3 marks available — 1 mark for every 2 suitable replacements)

Score Sheet

Fill in the score sheet after you finish each workout.

Write your scores below to show how you've done.
Each workout is out of 12 marks.

	Autumn Term	Spring Term	Summer Term
Workout 1			
Workout 2			
Workout 3			
Workout 4			
Workout 5			
Workout 6			
Workout 7			
Workout 8			
Workout 9			
Workout 10			
Workout 11			
Workout 12			